FUTURE SAVVY

FUTURE SAVVY

Identifying Trends to Make Better Decisions, Manage Uncertainty, and Profit from Change

Adam Gordon

HarperCollins
Leadership

An Imprint of HarperCollins

Future Savvy

© 2022 Adam Gordon

All rights reserved. No portion of this book may be reproduced, stored in a retrieval system, or transmitted in any form or by any means—electronic, mechanical, photocopy, recording, scanning, or other—except for brief quotations in critical reviews or articles, without the prior written permission of the publisher.

Published by HarperCollins Leadership,
an imprint of HarperCollins Focus LLC.

Any internet addresses, phone numbers, or company or product information printed in this book are offered as a resource and are not intended in any way to be or to imply an endorsement by HarperCollins Leadership, nor does HarperCollins Leadership vouch for the existence, content, or services of these sites, phone numbers, companies, or products beyond the life of this book.

Bulk discounts available. For details visit:
www.harpercollinsleadership.com/bulkquotes
Email: customercare@harpercollins.com

ISBN 978-1-4002-3254-3 (TP)

*For my parents,
Loraine and Gerald Gordon*

Contents

ACKNOWLEDGMENTS ix

INTRODUCTION 1

CHAPTER 1: Recognizing Forecast Intentions 17

CHAPTER 2: The Quality of Information: 39
How Good Is the Data?

CHAPTER 3: Bias Traps: 61
How and Why Interpretations
Are Spun

CHAPTER 4: Zeitgeist and Perception: 83
How We Can't Escape Our
Own Mind

CHAPTER 5: The Power of User Utility: 105
How Consumers Drive
and Block Change

CHAPTER 6: Drivers, Blockers, and Trends 133

CHAPTER 7: The Limits of Quantitative 153
Forecasting

CHAPTER 8:	A Systems Perspective in Forecasting	173
CHAPTER 9:	Alternative Futures: How It's Better to Be Vaguely Right than Exactly Wrong	197
CHAPTER 10:	Applying Forecast Filtering	215
CHAPTER 11:	Questions to Ask of Any Forecast	263
FURTHER READING		285
INDEX		289

Acknowledgments

Forecasts and future studies are a tremendous resource, and using them well is a key component of success. The future is important to everyone, and given how many forecasts are available in all fields, many for free, it's odd that so little has been written about evaluating them. Somehow, people think that "predicting is impossible" then blindly follow predictions anyway. I've repeatedly asked myself if and how one can bring "quality control" to the field; I've written this book to sort out my own thinking and to offer whatever benefit accrues to those who find themselves interacting with forecasts and wondering if, where, and when they are valuable.

Despite the little there is published, I have stood on the shoulders of giants. The work of J. Scott Armstrong and the Forecasting Principles Web site (forecastingprinciples.com) is an immense resource, particularly for technical forecasting. Steven Schnaars wrote a book about myths in technology forecasting twenty years ago, which Bob Seidensticker has expertly updated, and both have significantly guided me. Former colleagues John Mahaffie and Andy Hines have published seminal essays in forecast assessment, as have Laura Gibbons-Paul, Neil Duncan, and Martin Wachs. I find myself also referring constantly to the work of Gary Hamel and C.K. Prahalad, Edie Wiener and Arnold Brown, Kees van der Heijden, Art Kleiner, Paul Shoemaker, Jerome Glenn, and Ted Gordon in learning how institutions may develop foresight in valid and valuable ways. I'd further particularly like to thank Peter Bishop of the University of Houston who has been my teacher and mentor in the future studies field over many years. The errors in approach are of course my own.

I'd like to record thanks to the American Management Association and AMACOM Books for valuing the idea behind the book, and pushing it to completion, particularly Stan Wakefield for finding me on a teaching stint at INSEAD and convincing me to turn some theoretical concepts into pages that can be banged on the table; Barry Richardson and Erika Spelman who deftly ushered the manuscript through the editorial phases; Chris Murray, who worked fabulously on a first draft; and Kathy Whittier, who copyedited the manuscript and handled prepress production details.

Many thanks also to my wife, Helena, who edited the manuscript, showing once again what a remarkable intellect she is—a good, tough editor in text as in life. One of her more printable margin comments was "Dog's breakfast . . . Grrr".

Adam Gordon, May 2008

Introduction

THIS BOOK IS ABOUT HOW TO EVALUATE FORE-casts and extract value from them. It is written to help decision makers in commercial, policy, and nonprofit sectors, as well as ordinary people in daily life, make better judgments about predictions they read and hear, so they can appropriately plan for and profit from the future.

Predictive statements are all around us: in the newspapers, on TV, at conference presentations, in industry reports, consulting documents, think tank studies, and so on. All claim to be valid, but the record shows that few are. So while forecasts are a crucial decision-success resource, they are not in themselves valuable. they are only valuable alongside a clear way to separate the wheat from the chaff. What's valuable is being able to critically judge this torrent of information and to be able determine which ideas are worth taking seriously—worth planning for and investing in.

This book sets out to communicate tools and approaches that the forecast *consumer* can use to filter and evaluate statements about the future and thus judge what the real threats and opportunities are. It summarizes and orders the problems common in forecasting, as well as best practices, so that managers and decision makers of all types may be better able to critically interact with the barrage of forecasts that compete for their attention and resources and discriminate between worthy and unworthy ones.

Teaching a Donkey to Talk: Why Forecasts Can't Be Trusted

There's an ancient Uzbek parable about a con man who promised a local nobleman he could teach a donkey to talk—for a large fee—but it would take twenty years. Of course, in twenty years the con man, the nobleman, or the donkey would be dead.[1] Predicting is safe for the same spurious reason. By the time outcomes emerge, there is almost never anybody around to say, "Hey, that never happened!" And even where there is anyone who remembers the tarnished pearls of predictive wisdom, there is of course no penalty for being wrong. There's no skin in the game. The predictor may feel a twinge of embarrassment perhaps, but then, who can get it right all the time?

Not only is there no recourse, but putting predictions out into the world is ridiculously easy to do. Anyone can read a few articles, gather the direction of technology and social trends, and make projective links. The forecasting field is not regulated. There is no accepted conceptual framework, accepted methods, agreed professional standards, or guidelines for application to policy or business decision making.[2] There is no oversight board or council or licensing mechanism, no organization to which one must belong, no minimum qualifications, no agreed or standard curriculum in teaching forecasting. Anyone with a keyboard or a microphone, it seems, is welcome to babble on about digital media or nanotechnology or climate change or any other hobby horse, and before we know it, we are knee-deep in predictive wishful thinking, scaremongering, or blatant self-promotion, much of which is not worth our attention.

Part of the lack of standardization means there is no agreed definition of terms. In this book, I've used forecasting, foresight, predictions, and future studies more or less interchangeably to refer to works that look to and try to interpret the future. Some analysts use "forecasting" to refer to technical mathematical approaches, and "foresight" to refer to more impressionistic approaches.

Why We Don't Ignore Forecasts: Why the Future Matters

Rapid change is a constant, ubiquitous feature of our lives. We have seen eye-popping developments across society, technology, institutions, and products and services in the last generation; this will surely continue into the future. But change is not merely interesting. *It is competitive.* This is because success always implies congruence between decisions and the world in which those decisions play out. If we decide today to launch a product, buy a house, study for a degree, build a new light rail system, or take any similar decision of significance, the environment of tomorrow will be a key factor in the success or failure of that decision. What we do will be tested by the future conditions that emerge. Where there is a good "fit" between the initiative and the environment it plays out in—"the right product at the right time"—

> We have seen eye-popping developments across society, technology, institutions, and products and services in the last generation; this will surely continue into the future.

we can expect success. If not, we should expect to fail. Our decisions are only as good as the view of the future they rest on. All opportunities and successes and profits are realized in the future. All threats, failures, and losses are in the future.

In a fast-moving world, we know that the future environment will be different to that of today in big or small ways. New technologies, market shifts, changes in legislation, or evolving social values damage or destroy the traditional good fit we have between ourselves and the world. To achieve "future fit" we therefore use forecasts to position ourselves and our organizations, creating (or renewing) the fit between our initiatives and environment. In some cases we may be strong enough also to influence future events and outcomes for our own future benefit, and forecasts help us do this too. Either way, the earlier and clearer we see future circumstances, the better we will be able to benefit by changing our current recipes for success to keep up with the changes in the world. The better managers' view of the future, the better their decisions will turn out to be.

All enterprises benefit from narrowing down what they must adapt to and plan for—all effort spent preparing for a future that will not emerge is a waste of personal or organizational resources. Good forecasts are a key ingredient in limiting the vagaries of uncertainty, and therein working smarter not harder, avoiding surprises, exploiting new opportunities and plugging weaknesses in fitting in with the future, and where possible influencing the future to suit the organization. This is true not only of business. People and institutions of all types position themselves for success by anticipating and adapting to events, or shaping them. Whether it is an NGO raising money for developing-world children, an urban planner advocating a light rail system, a homeowner deciding to sell a house, or a student making a career choice, identical principles apply—a higher-quality reading of the future operating environment in which these decisions will play out is what separates winners from losers. We should all be vitally concerned with forecasts as we are all effectively betting significant resources on their validity.

So, as individuals and organizations, we are all faced with the task of grappling with the changing world under competitive conditions. Little surprise, then, that we appear "hard-wired" to seek information about changing circumstances and manifest a desire to peer ahead or absorb the insight of those who do. To be competitive we must be reading and listening to forecasts and factoring them into our world view and our plans. We cannot afford to ignore the forecast chatter. This is compounded by the rapid growth of information. The days of the panoptic amateur intellect are over. There's just too much to know in too many specialized fields. Whether we need to consider decisions concerning the future in healthcare, transport, education, or any one of a thousand areas, we find we are often required to call on specialists in those areas. Being forced to build our picture of the world on the expertise of others, we are, whether we like it or not, retail consumers of others' forecast perceptions.

Where the Forecasts Come From

Based on these factors, demand for predictive information and insight should be huge, and is, judging by the amount of news and consulting media generated that predicts technologies, innovations, legislative, social, and market change. Our appetite for prediction is willingly fulfilled many times over by an industry of prognosticators, forecasters, futurists, economists, sociologists, journalists, financial advisors, market researchers, defense and security planners, technology gurus, and every conceivable form of consultant and analyst. Sometimes this is called industry foresight or future studies.

Mostly it goes under more conservative labels such as economic analysis, market research, technology assessment, or competitive intelligence. National and international agencies such as the *U.S. Congressional Budget Office*, the *National Bureau of Economic Research*, the *IMF*, and the *World Bank*, to name just a few, are among the many bodies researching trends and publishing forecasts. Military and allied bodies, including the CIA, are deeply in the business of anticipating technology and global change and are publishing predictions in the public domain.

Every business sector produces and uses forecasts—for example, in quarterly or annual sales forecasts, tracking changing consumer lifestyles, or anticipating new technologies. Most major corporations keep a foresight unit going, and many—such as *Royal Dutch Shell* and *Siemens*—actively disseminate foresight. Management consulting firms, including the "big 6," trade on their reading of the future, as do fund managers and investment advisers. Forecast material is proliferating in industry research agencies such as *Gartner* and *Forrester,* which produce and sell predictions on every major industry. Foresight is a growing proportion of the business and general media, particularly in the print media, which—beaten to the news punch by TV and electronic media—is forced into off-news analysis. Magazines, from the general to the technical, are constantly interviewing experts, reviewing research, or revealing new-generation products to help the reader know "what's coming next."

> *What this translates into is an inundation of forecasts and predictions—whoever we are and whatever field we are in.*

What this translates into is an inundation of forecasts and predictions—whoever we are and whatever field we are in. The report is on your desk says "the recording industry will grow by 15% a year for five years." Your technology blog says, "nanotechnology will lead to desktop factories." Financial consultants advise that "the national debt will engender more volatile currency swings." Climate activists say, "the next war may be fought over water." The media says, "social security will be gone by the time we get there." A trend spotter says, "cars are the new office." Medicare says, "infometrics will allow more home-based elder care," and so on and so on.

There is no doubt that these and many other trends are upon us, that they will have short and long-term implications for policy and business decision makers, and that a correct reading of their outcomes will separate the winners from the losers. But, given what we know of the mixed track record of forecasting, how much of any forecast can we reliably depend on? On the face of it, any one prediction is as good as the next—certainly if you believe the forecasters' own claims to excellence. There's much at stake. Good quality forecasts are clearly valuable beyond measure, but the question in every case is: *Is this a good forecast?*

Some forecasts will be useful. Some will be junk. Some will be actively trying to influence future outcomes in their own interest. We cannot rely on them, but it is fatal to ignore them. We need to be able to examine and challenge forecasts, recognizing and discounting innocent exaggerations, deliberate lies, technological overenthusiasm, spokesman spin and salesmanship, and mechanical modeling—among the many pitfalls that the innocent forecast consumer is liable to fall into due to forecaster incompetence, or mischievous or downright cynical.

Predicting Is Poorly Done

Our competitive need to anticipate the future is matched only by our lamentable inability to forecast it. The record of future prediction is littered with the most astounding mistakes. From underwater cities never built to rocket mail that never flew to Y2K disasters that never materialized, the list of laughable errors is a mile long. With the benefit of hindsight, one is left wondering how sensible people—often experts in their fields—could have confidently anticipated things and events that didn't emerge while missing what was happening right under their noses? More often than not, a forecast is not just a poor analysis, but is clearly based on an entirely wrong-headed judgment about the status quo and the forces affecting it.

Bad forecasting is so ubiquitous that there are books and Web sites that catalogue (and smirk at) these failures. These lists showing up forecasters and industry "experts" correctly put us on our guard. But, as discussed in the next chapter, what these lists often miss is that many forecasts are *not* meant to be an accurate anticipation of events. Many are trying to influence the future, talk a particular outcome into being or shape it, or stop it from happening. People make predictions to sway an audience, or get a response from authorities or opposing forces. Forecasts are often salvos in the games of power and influence, flagrantly used to promote self-interests, in situations where accuracy is an afterthought.

> What forecast-failure smirk lists also miss, or underplay, is that a poor prediction often represented the widely held and generally affirmed "knowledgeable" position at the time.

What forecast-failure smirk lists also miss, or underplay, is that a poor prediction often represented the widely held and generally affirmed "knowledgeable" position at the time. It may be attributed to an individual, but that individual was merely the mouthpiece for common wisdom. This suggests that the failure of foresight is not the idiocy of individuals, but a more difficult problem. The sobering reality is that even the best "neutral" foresight work in the best institutions also often turns out quite wrong. Even where future analysts work competently and diligently, with balanced intention, the extreme complexity of human and natural systems makes medium- and long-range views of the future extremely hazardous.

What's instructive, also, is that the particular forecasting method doesn't appear to make a difference to correctness of prediction. The consistently poor quality of forecasting is not the problem of any particular forecasting technique. Whether it is trend extrapolation or Delphi studies, other forms of expert polling, impact-analysis, or statistical modeling, no method escapes failure, and they all appear to fail equally. This in itself suggests something crucial. Perhaps it can't be done, or at least not in the simple sense of "getting it right."

If all this is true, and proved in the poor record of forecasting, why bother forecasting or paying attention to future-oriented analyses? It is a short step to ignoring all predictive comments, saying, "I'll worry about it when it happens." Forecast skepticism of this type is quite common. The skeptic does not say the future is unimportant, just that we can't know it, and we should best deal with the unpredictable future by carefully monitoring developments and maintaining a high degree of flexibility, so that we are "ready to pounce" as necessary, as soon as the new situation demands it, rather than spending time and money chasing shadows or preparing for a "maybe" situation.[3]

Learning from Forecast Success

From skepticism it is a short jump to the lazy belief that we can know *nothing* about the future, and therefore can do nothing to respond to it or to shape it. That is a recipe for being caught napping. If we use personal or organizational success as a yardstick, it is clear that some forecasters or institutions or individuals do seem to have or have had effectively excellent foresight. They were somehow able to anticipate events in a way that was "good enough" to be very useful. In business, forecasting success is proved retrospectively by profit. There are of course many sources of profit, but one key element is having had the foresight to put resources in the right place at the right time, implying that decision makers had insightful views of future market or technology or social circumstances.

Regardless of whether they choose to publish their forecasts at the time—most do not for obvious reasons—successful foresight can be seen in every successful organization, such *Microsoft, Southwest Airlines,* and *Wal-Mart,* where winning has come from having anticipated the important trends in the world and in their industry before anyone else, or at least in time to maneuver their companies to benefit by creating appropriate products, services, and solutions. While *Pan Am* was missing the future, Herb Kelleher at *Southwest* was getting it. While *IBM* was missing the PC future, Bill Gates was getting it, and so on. Similarly, Henry Ford was able to foresee a mass market for automobiles before anyone else when he formed his motor company in 1903. Such good enough quality foresight can be seen in the success of organizations such as *Amazon, Capital One, Nike,* and *Nokia,* along with hundreds of thousands of smaller, untold stories where success came from having anticipated change correctly, or correctly enough. They didn't trumpet their view of the future. And they surely didn't see the future in perfect detail. But the outline was there, underpinning the strategic choices that they made in the evolution of billion-dollar businesses. Forecast success is, in fact, all around us.

In the public realm, successful foresight is often seen not only in benefits gained but losses avoided—the invisible nonoccurrence of crises, for example, in transport systems built in time to avoid gridlock, health initiatives that have offset epidemics, or development initiatives that forestall population explosion and/or famine. In a famous case in the 1960s, Singapore's Lee Kuan Yew saw emerging conditions that would allow Singapore to become a high-technology center of trade and industry in Asia. As a result, he set in motion policies that turned the country from a colonial swamp into one of the highest average-income cities in the world.

Of course, in these foresight-success cases, players were not merely predicting the future: They and their organizations were acting to *influence* it, and particularly to fulfill their vision. (Future-influencing prediction is discussed more fully in the next chapter.) But no organization, no matter how powerful, can determine or significantly influence the future. Most have to adapt to it to a large degree, to created congruence with the future, and successfully doing this depends on foresight to judge the course and timing of new initiatives under uncertain conditions.

Forecast Filtering for Self-Defense

This book takes a middle course between an uncritical reliance on prediction and overcynical dismissal of it. Certainly, dumb forecasts are made every day, but we do not merely smirk at the blunders. Forecast errors are instructive. Why was *AT&T's* massive bet on picture phones (the ability to see the other caller) wrong, while forecasts for a huge market in cell phones right? Why were those who forecast oil running dry by 2000 wrong, while those who forecast hybrid-car systems and uptake in alternative fuel sources right? What are they doing? What are they not doing? What do we learn from this? How do these errors improve our ability to evaluate forecasts, and therefore anticipate and profit from change?

> By dissecting failed forecasts we can understand the common and repeated errors and shed light on avoiding weak approaches.

By dissecting failed forecasts we can understand the common and repeated errors and shed light on avoiding weak approaches. We aim to learn from other people's mistakes in order to establish filtering criteria for good forecasts and to be able to critically assess each forecast and to be able to extract what value there is, if any. Forecast consumers must be able to ask of every future-oriented claim: How credible is it? How accurate or biased? Which parts of it are worth integrating into my mental framework? Which parts should be part of our organization's preparation and planning and which can be discounted and safely ignored? Can I use this knowledge to further the goals of my institution? Can I base a decision on this with confidence?

The million-dollar question is: How? Is there a way to weigh the utility in a forecast so that we can know whether it is something to note or to ignore? What are the markers for this? Is such a thing even possible, or to what extent or under what conditions is it possible? There are, in fact, a number of clear quality filters, questions, and hurdles through which one can put a forecast. A summary of the problems to watch out for and filters to apply is provided at the end of the book and offers the reader a handy checklist when evaluating any particular forecast. Chapters 1 through 10 present the argument and examples behind this list: piecing together the elements that make forecasts reliable, developing critical antennae for the types of problems likely in a weak forecast, demonstrating what a good forecast should look and feel like, and therein offering a dependable approach to evaluating predictions.

Chapter 1 introduces the broad categories of forecasts, to illuminate forecast intentions, particularly distinguishing between forecasts with future-aligning versus future-influencing purposes. Chapter 2 deals with quality of information and data in forecasts, addressing and necessarily eroding a too-secure belief in data solidity and dependability. Chapters 3 and 4 consider issues in quality of interpretation and bias, perceptual and cognitive filters, and mental models of the world that obstruct our thinking and therefore our forecasting.

From here we move into determining the forces that drive and block change, and how forecasts deal with them. Chapter 5 deals with the role of value or "utility" in determining the direction and timing of future outcomes, and the following chapter takes this forward to consider problems in trend-based forecasting. Chapter 7 develops issues related to complexity and considers how all elements of the world are interconnected so that changing one element changes everything else—often in unpredictable ways. Chapter 8 explores the themes that have been developed so far to illuminate the uses and limitations of quantitative forecasting, and this leads to a discussion of approaches to forecasting based on developing alternative futures and scenarios in Chapter 9. Chapter 10 provides short worked examples of forecast filtering, and Chapter 11 thematically summarizes the points made across the book, to create a template guide to forecast filtering.

Taken together, the steps in this book aim to put you, the forecast consumer, in better command of the forecasts thrust in front of you, allowing you to interact critically with the predictive chatter you read and hear, so that when you come across yet another breathless article about the "latest new thing," you will have the tools to keep your head when all about you are losing theirs.

Notes

1. Quoted in C. Thuron, *In Siberia* (New York: Penguin Books, 1999), p. 131.
2. There are various generally accepted attempts to synthesize a coherent framework for the future studies field. These are W. Bell, *The Foundations of Futures Studies* (Edison, NJ:

Transaction Press, 1996); R. Slaughter (Ed.), *The Knowledge Base of Futures Studies* (Foresight International, 2005); and J. Glenn, & T. Gordon, *Futures Research Methodology, v2.0* (CD-ROM) (American Council for the United Nations University: Millennium Project, 2003.) The field is loosely held together by the World Future Society in Washington, DC (www.wfs.org) and the Association of Professional Futurists (www.profuturists.org)

3. The wait-and-see approach is categorically rejected by authors Gary Hamel and C.K. Prahalad, who argue that short-term thinking will not allow a business or organization time to develop and place itself to occupy the high ground in its industry in the future. Businesses, particularly, often need to go through extensive R&D or other procedures of creating or adapting key competencies, and proceed through rounds of product and market refinement, all of which takes time, and which therefore demands foresight. See Hamel, G. & Prahalad, P. *Competing for the Future* (Boston: HBS Press, 1994).

CHAPTER 1

Recognizing Forecast Intentions

THE FIRST STEP IN BUILDING A MODEL FOR EVALuating forecasts is to understand the types of forecasts out there. There are, of course, dozens of ways of classifying foresight material, but the most useful way, for forecast assessment, is to sort it by stated or implied purpose. Forecast intention can be seen in forecast period (length of time); fixed point prediction versus willingness to develop multiple possible outcomes; overall author orientation toward optimistic versus pessimistic outcomes; and intention to either align with or influence the future.

Forecast Period: From Next Year to the Next Millennium

There are no agreed definitions, but in practice, forecasts of the future will fall into one of five categories:

- **Short-term forecasts** are focused on immediate change, normally zero to one year ahead. These are bread-and-butter operational forecasts used in day-to-day planning, supply chain and inventory management, anticipating sales numbers for the next quarter, or in budgeting. Most financial indicator forecasts—of inflation rates, GNP, trade balance, etc.—are short-term forecasts.

- **Short-medium forecasting** is, on average, one to three years. These are usually short-term forecasts extended to accommodate longer planning horizons within the operational sphere of a business or civil institution. The assumptions and methods used to make a six-month or one-year forecast are carried over to a longer time frame.

- **Long-medium forecasts** look between three and ten years ahead. Here, the operational purpose of forecasting gives way to broader strategic and other macro concerns. A company might use forecasts of this length to consider strategic changes in its industry, new competitors, new technologies, and new markets. These forecasts influence R&D directions, major capital investments, mergers and alliances, and the next generation of products and services. In policy or government circles, long-medium forecasts are used in considering technology and social shifts and changing infrastructural needs.

- **Long-term forecasts** look ten to twenty-five years ahead. Here, there is still some conceivable usefulness in organizational planning and decision making, but it is slight. In practice, long-term forecast time frames are most useful in allowing managers to relax overly realistic frameworks and assumptions about the world, and "play" with seemingly impossible outcomes that might derive from fundamental transitions in technology and society. This mental freedom may lead to worthwhile strategic discussions or outside-the-box thinking.

- **Ultra-long term forecasts** are anything from twenty-five to 10,000 years. Forecasters in this area put themselves outside any common business, policy, or institutional frame. Their concern is more philosophical and existential: to explore possible long-range futures for humanity, including its transformation. In this time frame, future thinkers are free to dream of ideal societies and perfect institutions, world (or intergalactic) peace, and other aspects of human (and trans-human) potential. Despite being the province of dreamers, and therefore not taken seriously, future thinking of this type, like science fiction, may lead to ideas that may filter into the mainstream. Forecasts very often take on the role and character of social commentary: posing utopias or dystopias against which society is invited to measure its progress.

These time frames are general guidelines. The balance between what counts as a short-term or a long-term forecast depends on the general rate of change in the underlying industry or topic area. For example, the electronics industry moves much faster than the mining industry, so a three-year forecast for "wi-fi" may be long-term view, while a three-year view of the Canadian mining industry may be a short-term view. The critical juncture is less at an exact time frame than at the point where forecasts concerned with operations give way to forecasts concerned with direction—the territory of strategy. In a fast-moving, turbulent area, an operational future would be no more than a few months, and three years ahead would be a strategic view. In a more slow-moving industry, a three-year view may be considered the operational horizon.

Short-term forecasts usually take existing structures, markets, competitors, legislation, and other parameters, as given, and forecast by statistical projections. A company may forecast for the year ahead—for example, by identifying which channels, market segments, price points, and value chain configurations will be most profitable—without questioning the nature or existence of industry or competitive factors, and without expecting them to change. The purpose is to fine-tune position to near-term industry and market conditions.

The short-medium and long-medium time frames are at once close enough to affect present decisions but long enough for the operating environment to change fundamentally. In these time frames we typically face hard, open-ended questions such as: How should a new technology affect our production decisions? Should we focus or diversify, or go abroad? How is the competitive environment changing? What policy changes will be required because of changing demographics, immigration, security requirements, etc.? The future at this level is more uncertain; therefore, a more wide-ranging, open-ended consideration of possibilities is required, one where causes of change are wrestled with and complexity is respected.

As we will see in the coming chapters, linear outcomes cannot be taken for granted beyond the short term. Longer-term horizons put us in a situation where much that we base forecasts on—our base of assumptions—will almost certainly change. Longer forecast period length is one of the factors that makes for analytical situations of high uncertainty and complexity, where the limits of trend-projective methods are reached. Therefore, the length of a forecast is a good indicator of the kind of approach that should be used and gives us a good indication of when a trend-projective or quantitative forecast is likely to have overstepped its realm of competence.

Point Forecasts Versus Alternative Futures

Classic forecasting is uncomplicated in its goal, which is to predict the future–that is, to determine what will happen and when it will happen, or, where faced with uncertainty, to find reason to prioritize expectation of one outcome over others. But, as we have seen, this "point forecasting" is very difficult if not impossible to do, particularly in high uncertainty situations or over long periods. The record of point forecasts is dim indeed.

In response to these failures, another view of what a forecast should be and do has grown up that backs away from the idea of a fixed prediction and, moreover, away from the idea that there is a "predictable future" that we can work out. Acknowledging the unfathomable complexity of human and natural systems, and our inability to know or compute all the variables no matter how hard we try, this approach instead adopts the concept of "multiple futures" or "alternative futures," and aims merely to identify the spread of possible and probable outcomes, without vouching for any one.

As the foresight success examples given in the previous chapter show, one way or another, many people and organizations are getting the future "usefully right" enough of the time to create profitable situations for themselves, despite taking long-term views. Therefore, perhaps, we don't need to get the future exactly right to be successful. Just going in more or less the right direction, at the right

> *Therefore, perhaps, we don't need to get the future exactly right to be successful.*

time, with the right assumptions, is competitively empowering. A flexible and hedged view of the future that is "somewhat correct" is obviously more useful to more people than a wrong prediction however singularly asserted.

The multiple futures approach goes for this lower, more realistic bar. A good forecast is not necessarily a "correct" one, or the one that convinces us of the correctness of one path. Instead, it is one that identifies emerging issues and potential events and prepares us mentally and organizationally for various scenarios and surprising twists of fate. In the alternative futures view, the test of a worthy forecast, therefore, is whether it has illuminated the unknown while shaking our assumptions, forcing us to clarify our thinking, stimulating and structuring difficult discussions, and getting us to ask the right questions and face the hard choices required to adapt ourselves and our organizations to manage future change. A forecast is not good if it predicts the future correctly; it is good if it better prepares us for a future that is inherently uncertain.

Obviously, what is lost or fudged in this approach is the hard-nosed quest to determine what *will* happen in the future—with the payoffs such knowledge would provide. Alternative futures may even be seen as a "cop-out"—the last refuge of forecasters who know they are going to get it wrong anyway. The tools and approaches of alternative future forecasting and scenario planning are described in more detail in Chapter 9.

Future-Aligning Versus Future-Influencing Forecasts

Those who research and produce forecasts, those who invest in understanding trends and drivers of change, and those (including the media) who bring the forecasts and their implications to our attention, inevitably have reasons for doing so. Forecasts are, after all, acts of communication that require effort—sometimes enormous effort in research and modeling and writing—and they surely wouldn't exist unless they returned a benefit in some form to the forecaster or the forecast consumer. Nobody thinks about the future just for mental kicks: The point is to benefit from the knowledge by seizing opportunities or avoiding threats or by affecting outcomes in the world. Benefit can be sought at any level: on behalf of self, family, group, institution, country, or the world as a whole. Understanding the forecast "return on investment" will give us an important vantage point in assessing the merits of a forecast.

> Nobody thinks about the future just for mental kicks: The point is to benefit from the knowledge by seizing opportunities or avoiding threats or by affecting outcomes in the world.

In broad terms, forecasts can return two types of benefit. One is where an individual or group seeks to anticipate (or approximate) what is coming to be more aligned with it—to create advantage for themselves by taking opportunities and avoiding threats more quickly or more elegantly. The other is where an individual or group seeks to try to influence the course of events itself, to promote outcomes desirable to them and head off those they consider negative. We may call the first type of future interest "future-aligning" and the second type "future-influencing." Very often a bit of both is going on at the same time as forecasters seek to both align with and influence the future, that is, promote their own future success in both ways. But, essentially, future-aligners aim to work on themselves to be ready for the future, while future-influencers aim to work on the world.

While some very powerful institutions may be able to influence macro events to some degree, and some businesses do become powerful enough to influence their industry conditions—controlling prices or industry standards or legislation (via lobbying)—most competitive enterprises are future-aligning. They view the forces in the market and society and technology as outside of their control, see their ability to influence the future outside of their own organization as limited, and therefore see their primary role as anticipating realities that will be forced upon them. A future-aligning organization will use forecasts to determine the terrain of the future before their competitors and so make earlier and better alignment, which may take the form of creative explorations to identify new products, or searches for alternative opportunities for existing capabilities, and so on. As we have seen, in principle the greater the alignment between a decision and the context in which it plays out, the higher the likelihood of success.

In future-influencing cases, by contrast, forecasters operate on the other assumption: that they, or we, can change the world. As environmentalist Rene Dubos exhorted: "Trend is not destiny," and the history of revolutions shows that if enough people want to change the future, then it can be changed. Within the future-influencing perspective, humans have control over at least those parts of the future that are human-created or influenced. We are active agents in determining what will or won't happen, and the future will therefore be what we collectively, through our actions and inactions, choose it to be. The teenager sitting in his room does not need to try to predict whether he will pass his math exam the next day. In this situation he has influence over the future. If he studies and masters the material, he will pass.

Many forecasts obviously cannot change outcomes. Forecasting a sunny day tomorrow will not change the planetary forces that determine the weather. Forecasting a lunar eclipse or the next appearance of Halley's Comet will not affect if and when these events occur. If we want to see the comet we have to go to the right spot at the right time—that is, *align* ourselves with a future event. But human affairs, or any natural or biological system where humans have dominion, are different. Here predictions interact with the phenomena they predict. The forecast affects the outcome it purports to predict by creating expectation. That is, it becomes part of the system affecting the outcome. What people expect to happen, and what people want to happen or not to happen, directly affects what does happen. The expectations and desires or fears that a forecast sets in motion influences the actual future that emerges.

One may see the activity of future-influencing forecasting in, for example, the prediction of computers being unable to distinguish between the year 1900 and the year 2000, and consequently sending financial markets and transport systems and other critical apparatus into chaos. The anticipated Y2K disaster was a prediction that failed to materialize. But this was at least in part due to many companies and governments and militaries having been spurred into action by the forecasts, hiring programmers to recode vital systems before 2000, which clearly had some effect (how much we'll never know) in nullifying the disaster. The forecast itself became part of the mix of forces acting on the future.

Note that any particular subject matter can be the subject of either type of forecast, depending on how the forecast treats it. For example, a forecast of a United States where large numbers of citizens do not speak English could go either way. It could be a future-anticipating forecast, suggesting demographic shifts and resulting changes in necessary business product and marketing strategies. The message of the forecast would be: "This is what is happening; this is what you could be doing to take the opportunity or avoid the threat." But seeing large numbers of non-English-speaking U.S. citizens could also be future-influencing. The intention might be to galvanize people who may be scandalized by this outcome and to get them to support new policies designed to counter it, for example, with improved access to or subsidy of English as a second language teaching, stiffer tests of English for new citizens, lower quotas on immigration, or other similar measures. The message would be: "This is what is happening, and this is what we can do to stop it from happening. Play your part now."

Future-Influencing Actors and Their Goals

Future-influencing organizations are typically those with a social, political, or environmental agenda. They will evaluate trends and anticipate outcomes in the light of the interests they represent, or the broader interests of society and humanity, and attempt to influence the evolution of events on behalf of these interests. Therefore, the forecast is designed to affect our thinking on the evolution of an issue, to motivate us to take action to influence the future toward the preferred outcome—for example, from lobbying against a new tax, to marching on the World Bank, boycotting a retailer, picketing a factory, or creating an online petition against child labor, which will, according to the forecaster, make a desirable future more likely or an undesirable future less likely. The forecasters involved are activists, advocating on behalf of a cause or its interest groups. Their object of the forecast is not to accurately depict the future.

Future-influencing forecasts are also common in business settings. Product and product category forecasts are typically future-influencing—that is, when a company says "Everyone will have a wireless digital assistant" or "Virtual technology will allow remote real-time collaboration," for example, it is not predicting in any neutral sense. It is trying to talk its preferred future into being. Future-influencing forecasts are also typically used in in-company motivation. Here the CEO or section manager may paint a picture of an ideal future where the company and/or product does fabulously well, profits are high, and everyone gets rich. This is neither a most accurate or most likely forecast. It is a future-influencing visionary forecast, aimed at motivating staff to turn the ideal into reality.

Sometimes future-influencing organizations are powerful agents in a world that may use forecasts to shape the future by preparing the ground—softening up the public—so that there is support for or less opposition to an initiative. The infamous "weapons of mass destruction" in Iraq (implying future use of such weapons by a loose-cannon dictator hostile to Western interests) was this type of forecast. It created the conditions for public acceptance for the necessity of war, lives lost, and billions spent. Many propagandistic forecasts in history are of this future-influencing type.

It takes power to influence the future, but putting out a future-influencing forecast does not imply that the organization behind it is powerful. In fact, many would-be future-influencing forecasts are created by two-bit organizations. The key to power is harnessing widespread public support. By entering the public debate and harnessing the power of public opinion, any organization, no matter how small, can potentially influence the future. Therefore, a future-influencing agent will typically create and circulate forecasts and publish images of a projected future as widely as possible to raise awareness and influence opinions and to create a groundswell of opinion and motivation that can be guided toward influencing action. (An influencing forecast may have the purpose of motivating us to *refrain* from action, for example, not buying battery-farmed chickens or not driving a gas-guzzling car.) As we will see in Chapter 3, future-influencing forecasts are far more prone to bias because of self-interest in the forecast.

Identifying Aligning and Influencing Forecasts

We cannot say which forecast mode—future-aligning or future-influencing—is better. They are each used for different purposes. The key, in filtering forecasts, is recognizing which of these modes a forecast falls into. This is not always easy. Both acknowledge uncertainty in their predictions, and both may use the same predictive tools, from data extrapolation to Delphi studies to scenarios. Sometimes such forecasts are less easy to see for what they are when they are cited or summarized—in the media, for example—which may obfuscate the forecast's original purpose. And, of course, a future-influencing forecast will seldom admit its agenda. On the contrary, influencing forecasts are often dressed up in scientific or technical apparently value-neutral frameworks, to gain legitimacy.

There are three primary flags indicating a future-influencing forecast:

- First, is the forecast published? As we have seen, influencing the future requires getting mass participation or broad acquiescence, so a key component of future-influencing is getting the word out. In order to achieve their goal of influencing the future, visionary forecasts (dystopias or utopias) must seek to harness larger forces outside of the agent or organization, particularly the power of public opinion, in order to create pressure for change. Therefore, visionary forecasts are inevitably are always publicly available. The more publicity the better, as their authors seek publicity to create a groundswell of opinion for social or policy interventions that will create a desired future or head off a dystopic vision. By contrast, future-aligning forecasts are seldom published. Whether they are the fruits of personal re-

> *Influencing the future requires getting mass participation or broad acquiescence, so a key component of future-influencing is getting the word out.*

search or a company assessment, they are proprietary. They are to guide the future alignment opportunity strategies for the benefit of the individuals concerned. As one would not normally share information that is useful for individual or group benefit with competitors, forecasts are not shared. This is why future-anticipating forecasts, as competitive documents, are hard to find in the public domain—at least until they are out of date.

- Second, does it specify an external change agenda? Future-aligning forecasts often present various options for consideration without any one being clearly better or clearly favored by the forecaster. Sometimes a best option—a product to create, or markets to develop, in order to benefit from the future changes anticipated—is suggested. But the actions suggested are things the company or organization *should do within itself* to improve its alignment with future events. For example, in the light of increasing financial security legislation in the external environment, a forecast may continue to suggest to a company that it invests in different accounting and reporting systems. In a future-influencing forecast, by contrast, the forecaster inevitably asks the reader to act in a particular way in the external world. The "signature" of such forecasts is the broad call to action—to curb emissions, ban handguns, promote a zero-carbon footprint, lobby for new industry regulation, or whatever initiatives forecasters think will improve the future.

- Third, is it a forecast of extremes? The world is a mixed place. Sometimes in history things are on average a little better for most people, sometimes a little worse. The chances are very

> Future-aligning forecasts often present various options for consideration without any one being clearly better or clearly favored by the forecaster.

strongly that the future will have a mix of good and bad in it. A forecast that asserts nirvana or living hell is therefore unlikely to be correct, but very likely to be trying to motivate or scare us to action.

Forecast Optimists Versus Pessimists

The final major category difference among forecasts occurs in the basic cast of the forecast—whether it is optimistic or pessimistic (or, as it often works out, pro-technology change or anti-technology change.) Forecasters, even where they use much the same methodologies, look at the same sources, and consider the same time frames, end up with very different forecasts depending on whether they are inclined to view the situation positively or negatively.

Future optimists—sometimes called "techno-optimists" or "cornucopians"—are hopeful of good outcomes and a better world. The idea that technology and society are evolving to raise standards of living and general well-being is a founding idea of Western industrial society. Most of us act in the belief that new technologies and new modes of healthcare, education, or domestic living will make our lives easier, less painful, and richer on all fronts. Therefore, the future will be better than today; therefore, change is mostly a good thing, something to be embraced. Change suggests to us, rightly or wrongly, that we are "on the road" to a better world.

We anticipate change will cause some uncomfortable disorientation and adjustment, but assume this to be the necessary handmaiden of growth and progress that makes us on the whole richer and healthier. In fact, growth and change are often put forward as the solution to current problems. We think of our task as to stimulate, adapt to, and possibly shape change, rather than to stop it.

The benefits of change and progress are considered obvious enough that societies actively assist the evolution of technology, both in the form of public- and private-sector R&D grants and in the protection of intellectual property that may derive from the research. We often consider our new technologies competitively important enough to guard them as state or trade secrets.

However, not all societies or all parts of society have this belief. Technology change is often viewed with trepidation, as most obviously expressed in science fiction dystopias where humans evolve into mutant automatons in a nihilistic future wasteland. Certain religious and so-called fundamentalist ways of seeing the world are clearly set against change. And there is serious sustained criticism of the costs of "progress," particularly from ecological and environmental watchdogs.

Prophets of doom have been around in every culture since time immemorial. The biblical prophets predicted fire and brimstone unless we mended our ways, and this mode of forecasting has come down to our own era, where the same trope is directly recognizable. Forecasting pessimists, sometimes knows as "Malthusians"—that is, echoing the pessimistic cast of Thomas Malthus who in 1798 published his treatise on the fate of man squeezed between population growth and limited resources—are generally skeptical of change and inclined to point out the many things that could go wrong.[1] Dystopias are enduringly popular in our tradition. Every movie with cities firebombed and in cinders, or depicting a post-nuclear holocaust or post-any disaster wasteland with mutant rogues or rampant viruses patrolling the earth, is in this tradition.

For a Malthusian, growth and progress are not the solution, in fact they are often the direct problem. The poster child for modern Malthusianism is academic Paul Erlich, who authored *The Population Bomb* (1967) and many other studies that have predicted human and environmental disaster in the wake of overblown commercial and industrial development.

Malthusians call themselves "realistic" and Cornucopians "naïve," and the debate is never-ending. In a now famous story, an economist, Julian Simon, in 1980 challenged resource pessimism by publicly betting Ehrlich and two other environmentalists from Stanford that any $1,000 shopping basket of raw materials of their choosing would be less expensive (i.e., more widely and easily available) by 1990. The loser was to pay the winner the actual price difference. Ehrlich and partners gleefully accepted and staked their bet on chromium, copper, nickel, tin, and tungsten. In 1990 Ehrlich had to send Simon a check for $576.[2]

Obviously, neither mental cast is fully right. It turns out the industrialization of agriculture easily allows feeding of everyone on the planet—even as many people still starve due to political and economic forces. We have more oil than anyone thought, but access to it is also not straightforward. But we have not all died in a nuclear holocaust, terror strike, or microbe invasion. With some obvious hiccups, technological and other forms of progress have been mostly good for humanity, as techno-optimists claim. And chances are we'll manage all the future problems we face, including genuinely worrying issues such as global warming and loss of biodiversity.

On the other hand, man-made and natural disasters do occur. From wars to disease to human and environmental holocaust, we have seen it all and probably will again. Pessimistic forecasts have a critical role to play in picturing why negative outcomes are possible, and so scaring us or otherwise motivating us to do something about them before it is too late. Rachel Carson's 1962 classic, *The Silent Spring*, which warned of environmental degradation, is credited with raising the political will to enact legislation to prevent chemical industry multinationals playing dice with the earth. At the time, techno-optimists were little more than apologists for new chemical industry technology and underplayed its future effects, a characteristic that is just as likely to be found in techno-optimistic forecasts today.

Utopias and Dystopias: The Extremes of Future-Influencing

An optimistic or pessimistic forecast may be of the future-aligning type. But it is more likely that an obvious positive or negative agenda will be part of a future-influencing agenda, as discussed above, predicting the good ways things could turn out and how to achieve them, or the bad ways things could turn out and how to avoid them. At the extremes the forecasters will develop full-blown utopias and dystopias. Classic literary dystopias such as *Brave New World* (Huxley, 1932) and *1984* (Orwell, 1948) are famous futurist dystopias. As with all future-influencing forecasts, these were not predictions in the sense of making a genuine best approximation of a future reality. *1984* is obviously not what Orwell thought 1984 would really be like. Nor was it what he wanted it to be like—he didn't want his prediction to be accurate. It is what he thought it would be like if totalitarian political and social forces were not headed off. The book creates a dystopic vision in order to raise consciousness about totalitarianism at a time when communism was still very much in fashion in Europe. In all similarly dystopic future-influencing forecasts, the authors do not wish their forecasts to come true. They anticipate a future in order to countermand it.

> An optimistic or pessimistic forecast may be of the future-aligning type. But it is more likely that an obvious positive or negative agenda will be part of a future-influencing agenda

Current environmental dystopias center on global warming, climate change, genetically modified food, and lack of species biodiversity, among other things. Forecasters anticipate negative outcomes, rightly or wrongly, and call on the public and policy makers to intervene. Utopias or "visionary futures" work in a similar but opposite way. Here a forecaster creates a vision of a better or ideal future, comparing what might happen (alternative futures) against the forecaster's preferred outcome. Articulating the vision helps clarify and focus the better future, in order to motivate anyone who supports that outcome to help bring it about. As with dystopias, the utopist vision is not what the forecaster thinks will happen, it is what he or she would like to see happen.

When Visions Collide: Power and Politics

Nobody will argue with the future-influencing vision of clean air and water and food for all. But that is more or less where it ends. Different stakeholders, subcultures, ethnicities, classes or nations generally don't share the same vision. In fact, one group's vision is often another's dystopia. In *Mein Kampf*, Hitler predicted a 1000-year Reich—a future-influencing attempt to rally support to turn his ideal future into reality. Clearly, his utopia was others' dystopia. In this way, different groups with different interests will want different futures to come about and therefore tussle over how the future evolves, with one achieving its vision at the expense of the other or others. America's visionary future is Al-Qaeda's dystopia and vice versa.

> Forecasts are therein often less best approximations of what is to come than weapons in a fight over the future, and the forecast field is a heated place of suggestion and intrigue as forecasts play their part in the never-ending struggle over resources, position, and influence.

History is a clash of wills, and so is the future. As forecasts can influence the future, and the future is often competitive between groups, we should expect forecasts to play a part in this clash by providing competing models of the future and advocating one or the other. Forecasts are therein often less best approximations of what is to come than weapons in a fight over the future, and the forecast field is a heated place of suggestion and intrigue as forecasts play their part in the never-ending struggle over resources, position, and influence.

Notes

1. Thomas Malthus *An Essay on the Principle of Population* (1798). The book has sold more than 30 million copies.
2. Quoted in B. Durrant, "Commodity Predictions: The Future Is Uncertain." *The Daily Reckoning* (July 2007). See www.dailyreckoning.co.uk/commodities-trading/commodity-predictions-the-future-is-uncertain.html

CHAPTER 2

The Quality of Information: How Good Is the Data?

A **FORECAST COMMUNICATES INFORMATION BE-**tween forecaster and reader and is subject to the same standards of accuracy, truth-telling, and bias-control by which one would judge any communication. As we have seen, forecasts can be very different in methods and goals, but all forecasts lay claim to factual truth. Future-aligning forecasts will cite data in order to justify an expectation of a future outcome. Future-influencing forecasts will cite data to motivate the reader to support initiatives and therein move the world. Optimists and pessimists will both justify themselves with data.

Therefore, the quality of the data and its interpretation is our next consideration. When a forecast brings data to support its hypothesis and conclusions, we need to ask how diligently this data has been researched and presented, whether it is appropriate and relevant to sustain the point, and whether it has been fairly represented, fairly used (is there conflicting evidence?), and fairly interpreted. Poor forecasting starts with poor data or poor interpretation of data. Good foresight work is inevitably tied to good facts about the status quo and fair interpretation of trends from this. We cannot forecast adequately unless we know where things are today and the evidence of forces at work on today, which will lead to tomorrow.

This chapter deals with the various ways in which data, and particularly numerical data, can be less solid than it looks, even with the best intentions. Chapter 3 deals with interpretative lenses that the forecaster uses to choose, amalgamate, and understand the data, including active misrepresentation and misinterpretation of data, intentional bias and spin.

Why Numbers Aren't as Solid as They Seem

We live in a world that values numbers and statistics highly. Numbers are our proxy for facts about the world; they allow us to think about it in a concrete way and to measure the results of our actions or inactions. Almost without exception, policy decisions of any significance—from acting against greenhouse emissions to managing school curricula—are made or backed up by numbers. We determine infant mortality ratios to tell us about social development; we compute polar ice melting to judge global warming, and so on. Where we enact policies to solve problems and advance welfare, we measure success by seeing whether and by how much we have moved the data. We measure, count, and compute to yield data and we ask, What does the data say? What numbers would be preferable? How do we achieve those numbers?

Similarly, we assess businesses by measurements such as return on investment, product cycle times, or rate of "capital turns," and judge management by whether it pushes the numbers in the right direction. Business success is judged by numbers even in areas where numbers are hard to assess. The management "Balanced Scorecard," for example, pushes quantification deep into the nonfinancial aspects of a company.

But numbers, and the facts they represent, are never purely objective. Any marketer will tell you that the wording of survey or focus group questions greatly affects answers, and this is the tip of the iceberg. Every data point, however statistically valid its construction, contains human choices within it: choices about what is looked for, what is counted, what it is associated with, and how it is interpreted. Between one analyst and another or one time and another, different decisions will be made about what to observe, how to identify significant instances, which ones to count, how to measure, and how to calculate.

> Every data point, however statistically valid its construction, contains human choices within it: choices about what is looked for, what is counted, what it is associated with, and how it is interpreted.

Moreover, data are seldom created or presented purely for our benefit. They are more usually soldiers of advocacy, created or chosen in order to be marched into battles over agendas and resources. Purveyors of data very often selectively choose data points to support their point of view or bring others around to it, to draw attention away from a problem or toward a proposed solution, or to arouse or diffuse public concern, and argue for a proposed intervention or outcome.[1] As Joel Best, in his book *Damned Lies and Statistics*—the best modern text on an old theme—says, "all statistics are ammunition." And not only are "hard" data subject to political interpretation and manipulation, but this interpretation is often presented *via* the data to benefit from the natural "truth claim" that numbers have.

Issues in Data Quality and Reliability

There are a number of specific issues that can undermine the quality and reliability of data. These include:

- Data from secondary sources instead of primary sources.
- Out-of-date data.
- "Future" data that has been projected from the past.
- Nonrepresentative samples.
- Data based on questionable definitions.
- Surveys that can be skewed by the form of the questions.
- Hidden numbers that can change the conclusions of the forecast.
- General proficiency in math and the manipulation of numbers.

The rest of this chapter will look at these issues, beginning with the problem of working with secondary data.

Secondary Data

The best data is primary data—data researched and presented by the original researcher—and the best use is primary use. If, for example, the researcher is making forecasts about teenage pregnancy, it is ideal if she has been the one in the field talking to teenagers. The forecaster who has personally been involved in research is most likely to understand the subtleties in the figures and what constitutes fair use of the results.

However, in reality, forecasters almost never use primary data. There are two reasons for this. The first is it is difficult and expensive to obtain, in terms of both money and time. The benefit of acquiring primary data often doesn't outweigh the costs, particularly when forecasters feel they can rely on the figures researched by others. The second reason is that most forecasters, most of the time, are working toward seeing "the big picture." They are collecting and collating data from many sources in order to make overall inferences about where things are heading. Their focus may be teenage pregnancy one day, but missile defense the next day. For this reason, almost all forecasters use secondary data, and inevitably from more than one source. As a result, forecasters (and therefore the forecast consumer) are one step further from the source, and the methodological competence and intention behind data is harder for the forecast consumer to assess.

Good forecasts based on secondary data try to bridge this gap. The mark of good data use is when we are given more than just the number—when we are told something about the definitions, measurement, sample size and composition, confidence intervals, or significance levels behind the figures presented. In the best cases the data methodologies and assumptions are presented so the reader can make a critical judgment of the data-gathering methods and statistical processes. But mostly forecasters do not do this. Where a source is cited, the forecaster commonly just relies on its reputation in determining whether due process has been applied in data acquisition and verification and asks the forecast consumer to rely on this reputation in the same way.

These are the particular problems in the use of secondary data.

Detachment of statistical caveats

Statisticians are a careful breed. Almost all results are specifically couched within a range of possibility and a margin of error. But in the secondary citation of data, the confidence interval—the estimate of how likely a sample characteristic is to be representative of a population as a whole—may be dropped, with misleading results. For example, if personal insolvency rates "jump" 5.8% to 6.2%, with a confidence interval of ±5%, then nothing has happened. But detaching the figure from its range of error suggests a trend. It dissipates the subtlety in the data and overestimates the conviction of the statistician. A good forecast will acknowledge statistical caveats in the data set before using it to make inferences for the future.

Detachment of context

Data only makes sense in a context of other data, and without it a data point can be misinterpreted. For example, statistics show that Americans drank 668 million gallons of wine a year, up from 267 million in 1970.[2] That seems like a huge increase, a trend of immense consequence in determining a worrying "future of alcoholism." But the total population is relevant, as is the consumption patterns of alternative forms of alcohol. In fact, the U.S. population of 1970 was two-thirds what it is today, and consumption of spirits and beer has been flat or declined. In other words the growth in wine consumption points to a change within the market (for health and other reasons) in the context of a steadily rising population, and there is no indication that alcohol consumption is on the rise or that alcoholism can be validly forecast. The poor forecast often omits contextual data in this way.

Number laundering and "gossip"

Like the children's game "gossip," each time data is repeated, it is also liable to be disassociated from its original context and become a bit more mangled in the retelling. Best cites a case where *US News and World Report* in a 1992 article said: "Researchers suggest that up to 200,000 people exhibit a stalker's traits." (This is in itself a number that sounds factual, but is so fuzzy as to be useless—how many is "up to 200,000"? Also, which traits are exhibited, among what type, and how many traits in total?) As news media picked up the report, it somehow became 200,000 people *being stalked*. Next, a TV talk show host said there were an estimated 200,000 stalkers in the United States. Then an article in *Cosmopolitan* said, "Some 200,000 people in the U.S. pursue the famous. No one knows how many stalk the rest of us, but the figure is probably higher." [3]

Legitimacy through repetition

Once a statistic appears in popular currency enough times that "everyone has heard it," it often becomes disassociated from its source and takes on a life of its own. If we keep hearing that "40% of Chinese children are overweight," the fact of its repetition will give the number legitimacy, and forecasters will be more ready to cite it, assuming that somebody somewhere has previously checked it. As a number becomes common currency, it becomes more likely to be cited and harder to challenge, yet no more likely to be valid.

> As a number becomes common currency, it becomes more likely to be cited and harder to challenge, yet no more likely to be valid.

The media accelerator

All of these problems are exacerbated when forecast data is cited in the popular and business media. The basic economics of a free-market media operation, whether print, electronic, or online, requires a media outlet to strive to drive up users (readers, viewers, clicks, etc.). The more users it has, the more attractive it is to advertisers seeking that target market, and the more advertising the media source will get and the higher rates it can charge.

Therefore, editors prefer "newsy" data—surprising or disturbing numbers—particularly about issues that potentially affect everyone. Further, the conditions of media production—particularly the need for brevity and to hold reader attention—forces journalists to extract data from its surrounding context and caveats. The careful circumscription of claims that typically surround a projection in an original forecast are likely to be left on the cutting room floor as the reporter reaches in and pulls out the juicy bit. Further still, the effect of one person's selective extraction can then become exacerbated as it goes through the hands of various editors, or reporters for other media sources, who may further condense and summarize it, leading the forecast further away from its original scope and purpose. So a research institute may put out a carefully considered life-extension technologies study, which is a good forecast in itself, but by the time it hits the newsstand as "You may live to 120!" the data has been stripped of caveats, decontextualized, and overplayed, if not actively sensationalized.

Old Data

Data goes out of date. It goes stale more or less rapidly depending on the topic area or industry concerned. Demographic data may last generations, but housing starts will be out of date in a year. As a general rule in business and policy arenas, the world changes quickly and anything over five years old starts to smell. But, as gathering primary-source data is difficult and expensive and sometimes, particularly in less-studied areas or parts of the world, no further work has been done, old data is all there is. Alternatively, the data may be privately researched, and there for sale, but getting it requires an investment on the part of the forecasting institution. For one reason or another, forecasters may continue to use old information and may fudge how old it really is. Good forecasts will date the data and will adjust or discount inferences made on old data.

Projected Data

By definition there can be no data from the future. Yet it often appears that data about the future is presented in the forecast. So it is important to know whether a forecast is based on historical data (the forecast infers the future based on real data) or whether it is based on projected data (past data has been extrapolated to future values, which the forecaster is reporting). The difference is subtle but crucial. Despite the various problems discussed in this chapter, data based fully on past events is more reliable than any projection—which immediately demands attention to the projection method and its assumptions. The savvy forecast consumer must now ask not only how good was the original, real data, but also on what basis and with what choices has it been "futurized"? The projection introduces a second layer of human choices and potential biases that should be approached with even more skepticism than recorded data.

There is one particular exception to this. Projected demographic data is valid future data. For example, if we know how many babies are born this year, we know reliably enough how many 10-year-olds there will be in ten years' time. In this specific case, we have a carefully contained basis of projection and little scope for error.

Sample Validity

Sampling is central to statistics. It rests on the assumption that what is true of a random sample of the population is true of the population as a whole. Therefore, we need only test a sample, which is much easier and cheaper to do. But the pivotal question is whether the sample is in fact representative of the whole, such that the inferences drawn about it will also be true of the larger population.

In order for this to be true, the sample must be of sufficient size to adequately represent the population, which is seldom a problem. But the sample set must also be completely randomly chosen, and this is often a significant problem. In fact, few samples are perfectly random. There are almost always problems of self-selection, biased or convenience-based selection, or other kinds of nonrandom selection. The classic case of this is reader/viewer polls, which are quick to tell you that, for example, 67.81% of readers support the right to doctor-assisted suicide. In fact, 67.81% of *the type of reader who has the time and motivation to call in to respond* supports doctor-assisted suicide. Despite this crucial error, the survey looks and sounds factual, and the number may insert itself into our future thinking.

Definition Validity

No definition is absolute. Some definitions are not specific enough to be of value, and other definitions can become obsolete. The following are the major issues of definition validity faced by forecasters.

Loose definitions

The problem of definition bedevils all efforts at categorization. It is often a choice (and sometimes a debate) whether an observation counts as a valid data point. If there is, for example, a reported a rise in attention-deficit disorder, is there a clear and consistent way this problem is defined? Does everyone define and count an instance of ADD the same way? At what point does attention deficit become a "disorder"? Is this an agreed point? Similarly, illiteracy, anorexia, or a thousand other common concerns share this problem of definition.

This is related to hypothesis testing and what is known in statistics as "Type 1" versus "Type 2" errors. The analyst, in producing the data, is making a hypothesis about what is a valid case that should be counted. Type 1 hypothesis errors occur where the analyst mistakenly positively identifies a case (false positives). A Type 2 hypothesis error occurs when the analyst mistakenly fails to identify, and therefore excludes, a valid case (false negatives). A data inquiry with looser definitions will be more prone to false positives—more cases mistakenly counted. Tighter definitions will lead to more false negatives—valid cases not counted. If, for example, one is assessing alleged human rights abuses in North Korea, the definitional question may be "What is a human rights abuse?" A broad definition will find more cases than a narrower definition and will therefore be favored by those who want to see more instances, and vice versa. The scope of the definition therefore becomes part of the debate about the data itself. A broad definition would suit human rights activists; a narrow definition would suit North Korean officials.

> The forecast filterer should ask how broadly an important definition has been interpreted, what stance on the issue is implied in doing this, and if the breadth is reasonable and consistent with how most others would define it.

Human language is a very inexact medium, and there is seldom an exact definition to fall back on. The forecast filterer should ask how broadly an important definition has been interpreted, what stance on the issue is implied in doing this, and if the breadth is reasonable and consistent with how most others would define it.

Definitions across time

Forecasters develop a trend by comparing measures across at least two different points in time. If, for example, juvenile delinquency rates were 3% in 1970 and 6% in 2000, an analyst may be motivated to say the trend is to greater delinquency, and by 2030 we may expect double-digit rates, or worse. In fact, comparing numbers over time is fraught with dangers. It assumes that the way the number was defined and measured has remained the same as now, and the context and meaning of the number then is the same as now. What was considered juvenile delinquency was likely measured and counted differently a generation and a half ago. Our attention to the problem may have changed; therefore, we may be including (or excluding) more cases, thus producing results that may look like evidence of a trend but in fact are not.

Sometimes a change occurs because people or society as a whole thinks a problem is more (or less) worth studying and reporting on, therefore the attention paid to it goes up (or down) and we do more (or fewer) studies. As we pay more attention to an issue, we are more likely to see manifestations of it. Sometimes social concern leads to legislation requiring measurement that was not required before. For example, the Sarbanes-Oxley Act, instituted following the *Enron* and other corporate scandals, requires more financial reporting. It is possible that this increase in attention and measurement will lead to a "rise" in the number of fraud cases in the United States.

It's likely that in the mid-1960s not too many people thought there was significant harm in giving a case of Scotch whiskey to a good customer at the end of the year. Now that would be frowned on and fall outside our limits of how we define ethical business practices. Drawing the ethics line tighter, and being more concerned with incentive ethics and therefore more likely to report on it, we are likely to find more cases of ethical violations in the early twenty-first century than in the 1960s. We may then be tempted to say fraud is increasing, when in all likelihood it is decreasing due to changing mores and more oversight.

In other words, differences between data points need not reflect actual changes in social or natural phenomena. They may merely reflect differences in the way we measure, the amount of measurement, or changing definitions over time of what is a valid instance.

Unless we can clearly say that these factors have not changed over time, we cannot fully trust the relationship between the historical number and the present number or the trend line it suggests.

While changing measures and definitions over time cause problems, unchanging measures can also be problematic. The classic case is the measurement of consumer price inflation, which is measured by pricing a representative basket of household goods. But what is a representative sample? Over the past decade the relative prices of manufactured items and basic clothes have dropped markedly, while households are paying much more for intangibles such as medical insurance and education. The vexing question of what goes into the consumer price index, and in what way it should be updated, is the subject of much debate. But it is clear that a study of inflation that did not update the basket of goods to reflect what people are buying, and a changing balance of costs, would provide misleading numbers.

> *While changing measures and definitions over time cause problems, unchanging measures can also be problematic.*

Definitions across places and situations

A lack of standardization in definition across places and situations—different cities, states, countries; different legal and moral systems; and different research and reporting systems—also skews data. It is not clear that a survey of religious education in schools would be done the same way in Kansas as in Oregon, with the same definitional choices or the same questions asked in the same way. This difference would lead to studies that might not be directly comparable, and making direct inferences based on comparison of the data would be misleading.

Across cultural and international boundaries the problem becomes more acute. For example, the commonly cited "crisis" of U.S. K–12 education is made with reference to achievement in other parts of the world. Regardless of whether there is a crisis, there is undoubted variation in what defines success, which students are measured, and how they are measured. For one thing, many countries stream the lowest student tier into vocational training, effectively excluding them from academic achievement data.

Place also influences data-attention problems, and this particularly skews and often renders useless international development data. A country such as South Africa, which has generally good infrastructure and solid institutions of social and scientific research, consistently reports all kind of development problems, from AIDS to infant mortality to violent crime. They find these things because they are there, but also because they have the resources, ability, and political will to look for them and institutions with the research capability and statistical competence to report them. Going strictly by the data, one would be induced into a relatively gloomy forecast for South Africa, while thinking that countries in far worse situations have brighter prospects.

Survey Data and Delphi Studies

Surveys are a notoriously difficult area because the nature of the questions influences the responses given. Leading questions will create bias in the responses. Questions not asked will leave holes in the information. Better-quality survey design methods go a long way to eliminating bias from a question set, but there's no law to say these techniques must be used or have been used in the forecast you happen to be reading. Generally, surveys run by credible polling firms are more dependable than something cooked in-house. Forecasts based on survey data should publish the survey questions somewhere in the document, a good habit mainly honored in the breach.

Delphi studies are a form of survey particularly designed to elicit forecasts. In such a study, interviewees (often experts in a particular field) are asked to assess the likelihood and timing of forecast events put to them. Through various rounds of questions—where each member is individually questioned to avoid persuasive people swaying the group—the range of expected events and timing is narrowed, and data is created as to the average expected likelihood and timing of these events. Although a Delphi survey is attractive precisely because it quantifies expected likelihoods, Delphi surveys suffer the same problems as all surveys: Question selection and design deeply influences the results. Also Delphi numbers are mathematical averages of interview opinion. The numbers are not based on research into any facts on the ground.

The Politics of the "Dark Figure"

It is generally accepted that not all cases or instances of an issue are presented for counting. Due to practical circumstances, oversight, or political power, many cases are missed or hidden or otherwise go unreported in the data. Not all rapes are reported. Factories won't commonly report their own polluting behavior. These missing cases—the difference between official records and the true number—are known as the "dark figure."

> *These missing cases—the difference between official records and the true number—are known as the "dark figure."*

As time goes by, with enough research the figure can sometimes be estimated with some confidence (as with the Justice Department estimate that 61% of rapes and sexual assaults are still not reported.[3])

However, in the case of a newer social or technological issue, analysts will be required to guess at the existence and size of the dark figure. The less real evidence there is, the more the dark-figure guess will vacillate, and the more it will be a political number. Analysts will guess in the direction that serves their interpretation. Tuna factory ships surely don't report all dolphins and turtles and other mistaken fish they catch. An analyst arguing for international legislation to protect marine life would estimate the dark figure as high, while a Taiwanese fishing consortium would estimate it as low.

Innumeracy

The final common problem in forecast data has to do with basic innumeracy—a lack of skill or understanding of numbers. John Allen Paulos has written a number of justly famous books on innumeracy in everyday society and in the media and cites the common mistake of misunderstanding probability. If a person tosses a fair coin, most people can work out the probability of a "heads" toss as 50%. Fewer people can work out the probability of a heads toss if three people toss a coin once, or the conditional probability of, for example, two "heads" tosses if the first toss is a heads.[5] These may seem trivial examples, but forecasting routinely requires understanding common math principles—never mind complex mathematical modeling—and small errors of innumeracy and logic scaled up often result in hefty errors in published forecasts. Sometimes numerical confusion and incompetence are not easy to spot because the mistake may be well upstream of the forecaster. Sometimes a touch of common sense will ferret out a mistake. Joel Best cites a commonly quoted statistic of U.S. society: "Every year since 1950 the number of American children gunned down has doubled." (If this were true, the number of children gunned down each year would have passed one billion in 1980).[6]

Improper Use of Data

Sometimes the data itself is valid, but is improperly used either due to innumeracy or to interpretive bias (see next chapter). The main forms of improper use are the following.

Lack of adequate connection between data and inference

Here the data does not adequately or fairly connect to the inference being drawn, or only connects under certain assumptions, such that it doesn't necessarily or reliably point to the future that the analyst claims. If, for example, a rise in interest rates is cited as evidence of European economic decline, is this association correct? Are there additional, alternative, or even opposite interpretations and inferences? Sometimes, because of the cost or trouble in obtaining data, forecasters are drawn to using information that is easy to find, rather than that most relevant to the forecast at hand. This is like looking for one's keys under the lamppost. The closest or handiest evidence may not be sufficient to make the future inference.

Mistaking correlation for causation

Often two numbers are correlated without either one's being the cause of the other, and it is a mistake, whether intentional or not, to assert causation or future causation. For example, smoking, which causes cancer, correlates with low exercise, which does not cause cancer. It would be a mistake (in the absence of smoking figures) to base a cancer forecast on low-exercise figures. Similarly, being married and owning a home both correlate with creditworthiness, but neither is a direct cause of the other. It would be unreliable to use these indicators to assert future causation (e.g., that a rise in homeownership would lead to higher rates of marriage.)

Scaling assumption errors

Another classic error of interpretation, whether willful or not, is assuming results are automatically scalable. In fact, it is mostly not valid to scale up or down. If China's economy growing at 10% has produced 100 million entrepreneurs, it is not necessarily valid to say that if it grew at 15% it would produce 150 million entrepreneurs. Nor is it likely that doubling the amount of money spent in combating child prostitution would halve the number of girls on the streets. New factors and forces come with changes in scale, and these will likely prevent a scaled-up variable behaving in the way it does at its original scale.

Practicing Number Skepticism

Clearly, numbers are important, and no forecast should be without them. But all the issues and problems in the research and reporting of data tell us that no number is pure or true. While it is deeply ingrained in us that "numbers don't lie," in fact, every number and every factual data point is produced by and subject to human interpretation. That is, all numbers lie a bit, and some lie a lot. While data use suggests solidity and neutrality, and may appear above the fray of social and moral choices, all numbers and their interpretation sit on top of the shifting sands of human paradigms and intentions, influenced by our expectations and persuasions. Numbers are just as much social products as any other form of knowledge.

> That is, all numbers lie a bit, and some lie a lot.

Quantitative studies often come dressed up with complex equations or fancy graphics and multicolored 3D presentations, playing up the reliability of their number-based forecast methodology, and therein claiming due process. But no matter how scientific the data appears, choices have been exercised at every point about what to observe, what to count, how to measure it, and how to report it. These choices create the data, and different choices would create other data. Well-created, fairly used numbers are an excellent guide to current and future trends. But numbers are not bedrock. There is no bedrock.

Good data sets, based on clear, reasonable definitions and good samples (that is, valid inclusions and exclusions) and valid solutions to the problems identified above are also common. So, as with forecasts themselves, our problem is that data is of mixed quality, and it is hard to tell the good from the bad. The only defense of the savvy forecast filterer is to acknowledge this and make a concerted effort to understand what choices have been made in the data presented, and how fair these choices are, asking: "What might be the sources for this number? How could one go about producing the figure? How might the phenomena be measured, and which measurement choices have been made? What sort of sample was gathered, and how might that sample affect the result? Is the statistic being properly interpreted? Are comparisons being made, and if so are the comparisons appropriate? Are there competing statistics, and if so, what stakes do the opponents have in the issue?"[7]

It is usually difficult to evaluate primary data research or statistical analysis because the necessary background information, or access to it, is often not provided by the forecaster. But there are clues about the reliability of the data. If a data point or trend appears outside the spectrum of what is known about a situation or problem, for example, are there other sources that would verify it, by which one may "triangulate" the data? If not, there is a case for raised eyebrows. Also, it is helpful to assess whether the data is *used* in a balanced way in a forecast. If it is, chances are the forecaster is producing or choosing balanced data to use. If a reporting agency has no specific stake in the data one way or another—it doesn't benefit if a number is high or low, or is changed or unchanged—then there is no call to influence the data. If the data provided is clearly in support of one side of a debate or controversy–the number of gunshot deaths, amount of industrial water contamination, the rate of abortions, racism in the workplace–the savvy forecast reader should be more skeptical.

Notes

1. J. Best, *Damned Lies and Statistics* (Berkeley, CA: UC Press, 2001).
2. Figure provided by The Wine Institute: www.wineinstitute.org, viewed February 2008.
3. Best, op. cit., p. 36.
4. David A. Farenthold, "Statistics Show Drop in U.S. Rape Cases—Many Say Crime is Still Often Unreported." *Washington Post* (June 19, 2006).
5. J.A. Paulos, *A Mathematician Reads the Newspaper* (New York: Basic Books, 1996).
6. Best, op. cit., p. 2.
7. Ibid., p. 169.

CHAPTER 3

Bias Traps:
How and Why
Interpretations
Are Spun

THE PREVIOUS CHAPTER LOOKED AT PROBLEMS in quality and validity of data that may be presented in support of a forecast. In this chapter we consider how data—whether good or bad in itself—can be interpreted or misinterpreted in creating a forecast.

As established earlier, forecasting is done for the advancement of an individual, organization, group, nation, or humanity as a whole. This benefit can come in the form of anticipating change and aligning with it, influencing future outcomes to one's own advantage, or both. As we move to consider the interpretation of facts and data, it is these "political" aspects of forecasting that become central. The forecast filterer needs to take a clear-eyed view, recognizing that people rarely tell us anything out of the goodness of their hearts, purely to inform or educate us. And, just as there is no "value-free" look at history, so too there is no value-free look to the future. We need to ask who is talking to us about the future, why he or she is doing it, and what his or her agenda is, and be ready to mentally rebalance the forecast interpretations that are presented.

Natural Versus Intentional Bias

The key issue in interpreting data is bias—the ways in which the interpreter will, consciously or unconsciously, bring a personal or organizational preference to bear in selecting data or extracting meaning from it. But not all bias is manipulative and cynical. Even where a forecaster is using factually valid and technically accurate information, a point of view will always insert itself into the analysis. Two people with the identical information will not necessarily interpret it the same way or derive the same forecast from it. Pure objectivity is not possible, and interpretations of future possibilities from current trends and uncertainties can likewise never be objective.

> *Pure objectivity is not possible, and interpretations of future possibilities from current trends and uncertainties can likewise never be objective.*

This saves us from chasing a chimera. Natural bias is not necessarily bad, or an "error" to be corrected. It is inevitable. Everyone has a point of view. Also, forecasters are always shaping information, tidying it up, and glossing over weaknesses, often without realizing it. Accurate information is no guard against this. And everyone's observations and opinions are deeply influenced by his or her own culture, education, personal experiences, and contextual incentives. These interpretations are an inescapable product of the way forecasters see and organize the world, and the beliefs and preferences they bring to bear. The role of these perceptual frames and paradigms in creating natural bias are dealt with in Chapter 4.

However, at a certain point natural bias merges into an intentional, calculated act. A line is crossed where interpretation becomes something altogether more premeditated and manipulative—the intention to misrepresent the evidence on purpose, or to skew its interpretation, to lead us to a forecast conclusion that creates advantage for the forecaster or forecast institution. In future-aligning forecasts—where the forecaster has no particular interest in one set of outcomes over another—the bias is likely to be natural bias. By contrast, in the future-influencing forecast, the likelihood of conscious bias is far greater. A forecaster who sees personal or institutional benefit in a preferred future coming about, or a dystopia avoided, has clear motive to promote the necessary future-influencing perspective, while submerging alternative inferences and opinions on an "ends-justify-the-means" basis.

The following are the particular markers of intentional bias in forecasts.

- **Selective choice of data or omission of conflicting data.** Here data is quoted accurately but countering evidence or opposing numbers are not given. This is the oldest trick in the book, but that doesn't mean it is not practiced every day. It is often difficult to spot if you are not expert in the field. The only reliable way around this is to seek out forecasts on similar topics from people or organizations with different interests.

- **Prejudicial organization and emphasis.** Another standard technique is devoting uneven time or space to contrary evidence. By running one set of data more prominently than another, or by prejudicial organization, the forecaster is able to highlight supporting evidence or downplay countering claims.

- **Emotional words and evocative images.** Through use of word choice, emotive language and associations, or emotive stock phrases, the forecaster is able to promote one interpretation over another. If, for example, a forecaster says a new soup-kitchen policy initiative is going to be "soft on crime," he is reaching for a phrase that is evidence of likely bias in the forecast.

- **Letting worst-case examples stand for the whole.** Here an extreme fact or case is presented and, while true in itself, is falsely allowed to represent the general case. The author making a generalization from the one or two vivid instances implies the extreme is the norm. For example, a portrait of a genuinely psychotic soccer hooligan may be given, which we are invited to see as typical, and so accept the inference that a current or future problem is more serious than it actually is.

- **Prejudicial definition of key terms.** As discussed in the previous chapter, definitions always imply interpretation. Some forecasters define terms as fairly as possible, but others actively "spin" the definition of key terms, or choose the most profitable from among various definitions or labels. One person's "terrorist" is another's "freedom fighter," and this is true of terms used in forecasts, too.

Bias-Prone Context and Bias Traps

As we have seen, future-influencing forecasts are more likely to display intentional bias than future-aligning forecasts. Knowing this, it is helpful to recognize common future-influencing forecast contexts, which are typical bias traps, as listed below. Many of these are classic conflict-of-interest situations where forecasters are unlikely to be neutral.

One of the things bias-prone forecast contexts have in common is they are situations where there is very little cost in being wrong. Whether it is a business predicting big sales, a politician predicting nirvana, an NGO predicting disaster, or a newspaper predicting World War III, they are all united by the fact that there is little or no penalty for being way off base. The corollary is also true. A good indicator of forecast reliability is if there is cost to the forecaster, forecast organization, or publisher for being wrong. Does the forecaster have, as it were "skin in the game"? Anybody can wax lyrical about the future, but if there are real financial or other resources at stake, the forecaster will be much more circumspect.[1] As venture capitalist firms typically insist that entrepreneurs seeking funding have at least some of their own money invested in the new business—an indication of their belief in a successful result—so too it is a heart-warming indicator if there any evidence of real investment of resources of any kind based on the forecast. Actions speak louder than words.

> One of the things bias-prone forecast contexts have in common is they are situations where there is very little cost in being wrong.

Bias-prone contexts include the following.

Self-Asserted Forecasts of Success and Failure

Companies and their spokespeople are almost never neutral forecasters of their own future performance. They usually have a very obvious incentive to forecast the biggest and widest success that credibility will allow. Predicting their future success is a way of influencing the future toward that success, saying, "Sales will be big," "this product is about to take off," or "there's a $5 billion market for this drug," etc., is an attempt to create a self-fulfilling prophecy where more people think the product is going to take off, creating more interest in it, making it more likely to in fact take off. Similarly, company spokesmen may blithely inflate expected sales or market share to influence analysts, bankers, and stock market forces in a company's direction, or when raising capital or seeking support for a merger.

Sometimes negative forecasts of impeding failure or difficult market conditions benefit a business, particularly when (surprise!) the failure turns out to be spectacularly overcome. For example, a company may underpredict future sales or revenues in order to "manage" analyst expectations. Or future performance may be underestimated to offset antitrust actions or to blunt union demands. Often industry experts can refute unreasonable business or industry forecasts, whether positive or negative, but this is harder in new industries with new technologies where the future is more uncertain. The forecast consumer should be especially careful of forecasts of adoption of new products or new technologies, where the baseline of a credible forecast is less known and companies can make stupendous forecasts without being called to account.

Internal, Motivational Forecasts

Conscious bias also commonly exists in internal company forecast documents, where overoptimistic success predictions are aimed at an internal audience—to motivate management, staff, or industry partners. Similarly, a pessimistic internal forecast about new competitors, tightening industry conditions, expected regulation, and so on, may be circulated to frighten workers into working harder or not asking for a pay raise.

Our culture likes good news and positive thinking. Positive forward thinking—for example, forecasting healthy sales figures for the coming year—is subtly or overtly rewarded. We assume it goes with a "winning mentality." It may have motivational value, but doesn't mean the forecast is any more accurate. In the same vein, negative expectations are viewed as evidence of lack of winning intent; therefore, these predictions are often underplayed or not made, for fear of the consequences. Sometimes a negative forecast may result in penalties such as department closures, layoffs, or demotions, creating direct disincentives to make such forecasts. This all works to create internal forecasts of future success that are less credible than they appear.

Sometimes an optimistic "stretch" forecast policy will be part of routine company management, for example, where expected sales projections are pumped up because the incentives and bonuses of the sales force are tied to the forecast—a low forecast could lead to more people "making their numbers," and therein earning higher bonuses. Higher reference forecast projections make bonuses kick in later. Sales staff would obviously have incentive to bias the forecast the other way, to make the targets easier to reach.

Internal company forecasts of costs, sales, revenues, and market share are also fraught with in-company rivalries and succession politics. Forecasts may be created or manipulated to reflect creation or maintenance of company fiefdoms, to suit a personal or group agenda, to effect a promotion, to motivate for the amalgamation or separation of departments, or to spur or block the development of new products. In other words, the internal company forecast plays a part in the constant turf wars that beset organizations and is less credible for it. This is, of course, equally likely to be true of nonprofit organizations, where personal and group agendas may similarly not be above marshalling forecasts in the quest for a bigger slice of budget, expanding or contracting staff or entire departments, or affecting the direction of the institution as a whole.

Where Foresight Influences Funding

Most social and nonprofit organizations depend on research grants and direct donations to continue to do their work and, where possible, expand the mandate of the organization. A spokesman for every organization that seeks funds has a clear vested interest in making a forecast that safeguards the relevance of the organization's work now and in the future. That is, there is a clear incentive to forecast that the problem being tackled is going to get worse or at least continue to be a serious one. Therefore, these forecasters will be more likely to publish and promote worrying numbers or worrying interpretations. For example, if they were to forecast is that fish farming is safe, then no "worry money" would be forthcoming. But if they forecast "piscatory" spongiform encephalopathy, and set themselves up to address this problem, they are more likely to get their funding. People who work for good causes may have their hearts in the right place, but they also have their mortgages and their children's college fund in that place. They have to safeguard their own relevance, and the only way to do this with donors is to paint enough of a future problem in their area of concern to keep donor money flowing.

It is overly cynical to think forecasts are *always* biased in this way, but the conflict of interest is acute. When is the last time you saw a problem-solving institution forecast that the problem is going away? Whether it is forecasts of AIDS, carbon emissions, or child molestation, it is very likely that the institution will (while being careful to know the good and crucial work that has been done and perhaps suggest how much worse off we'd be for lack of it) more often than not suggest a growing concern for the future in their area.

Sponsored Forecasts

Often there is clear benefit to an organization in making a forecast, and so it pays for it to be done or publicized. Sometimes it is simple to tell that a forecast has been commissioned or sponsored by an organization, and as the adage goes: "The one who pays the piper calls the tune," so one may expect a deliberate interpretive spin on a set of facts to create a certain perception in the reader. Everybody knows this, which is why the fact of foresight sponsorship is sometimes disguised or hidden outright. Particularly common is the situation where a corporation will support a foresight project that is undertaken by a nominally independent research organization or think tank.

Election and Government Forecasts

Election candidates and campaigners are famous for broken promises, which come about due to poor, self-interested forecasts made by the candidate and swallowed by the electorate. The politician paints the rosiest possible outcome of proposed policies and initiatives . . . if he or she is elected (along with terrible outcomes if an opponent is elected). The incentive is not to give an accurate view of the future; it is to use a forecast of the future to get elected. Of course, the forecast commonly turns out to be hot air.

Similarly, when sitting governments, presidents, or bureaucrats find themselves in a jam, they may postpone the wrath of the public by reaching for forecasts. They often say something that approximates to "give our initiative more time to work and lead to a brighter future"—forecasting success at a future time to delay facing the music now. Forecasts are also used, often cynically, to create support for a new initiative. We need to think no further than widely published predictions by U.S. government and pro-war pundits that U.S. soldiers "would be welcomed into Baghdad with bouquets" to see how this kind of forecasting works.

Publicity and the Need for Extremes

We have seen that forecast institutions with a future-influencing agenda need publicity for their forecasts to attract and motivate the public to influence the future. The realities of competition for publicity are such that more extreme and outrageous forecasts are more likely to get more publicity. This creates the incentive to bias a forecast toward the extremes of what is likely.

This also works at a personal level. Many people in the forecasting world live by their profiles—the more renowned they are, the more and better work they get, and the higher the speaking fees they command. Once again, there's a conflict of interest. A sober forecast will not command attention. An extreme, revisionist forecast is a better gambit in the battle to get noticed. Any forecaster who seeks publicity is likely to be biased toward extreme future outcomes rather than the more-likely middle ground.

Insider Forecasts

Insiders in an industry or company often have a vested interest in the present and forecasting little change or downplaying change, which biases their forecasts. Insiders have typically built up their career based on expertise concerning the status quo. They derive their status and financial and nonfinancial rewards from their mastery of current systems. Their knowledge is bound up in what is going on inside their field and how to achieve within current systems and technologies. It is unlikely that such a person will be able to even-handedly bring him- or herself to acknowledge or legitimize likely alternatives. For example, a radiographer who has spent fifteen years specializing in his trade may vociferously resist the forecast that 95% of medical diagnostics may be automated by computers—with obvious implications for hospital budget allocation. Internal politics also plays a role. The old guard expert will be less likely to forecast anything that diverts resources and attention to a "young Turk" faction within a company and more likely to self-interestedly protect a current position by forecasting outcomes in such a way as to suggest that people "do their time" within current organizational structures.

For these reasons, there are distinct benefits of getting forecasts from industry outsiders, who have less investment in the status quo and less to lose from change. Outsiders are more likely to be willing to see change and are therefore more likely to see it and forecast it. Outsiders will also generally have more experience of forces and factors from other fields, or bring a comparative perspective as to how things have changed in other industries, and be willing to apply these analogies.

> There are distinct benefits of getting forecasts from industry outsiders, who have less investment in the status quo and less to lose from change.

The weakness of insider forecasts is true at an institutional level as well. You would expect *General Motors* to know the most about the future of automobiles, or *The Washington Post* to have the best insight into the future of media, and so on. Often these companies, or the trade associations they are part of, do spend considerable resources studying and anticipating change. But, as analyst Bob Seidensticker points out, the digital watch didn't come from established watch companies, the calculator didn't come from slide rule or adding machine companies, video games didn't come from board-game manufacturers *Parker Bros* or *Mattel*, the ballpoint pen didn't come from fountain pen manufacturers, and *Google* didn't come from the *Yellow Pages*.[2] New product and services almost inevitably come from outside an industry, where mental, financial, and infrastructural investment in the status quo is less of a factor.

Management academics Gary Hamel and C.K. Prahalad use the terms "managerial frames" and "corporate genetics" to describe the set of biases, assumptions, and presuppositions managers have about the structure of their industry, how one makes money in that industry, who the competition is and isn't, who the customers are and aren't, what customers want or don't want, which technologies are viable and which aren't, and so forth. As they point out, these frames will be tighter if there is a strong internal organizational culture—if, for example, people hired are from similar backgrounds or there are comprehensive employee induction programs or similar processes that promote alignment of thinking and perception. Tight frames make managers less willing to see and forecast change, particularly change coming from the outside.[3] The role of mental models and paradigms is discussed more fully in the following chapter.

Media Situation Biases

As mentioned in the previous chapter, the media plays a role in compromising the integrity of data. It also has its own particular interests and incentives in selecting and interpreting forecasts. Some media outlets exist to promote a particular cause, and they will select and adapt forecast material to reflect this bias. But even where a particular interpretive line is absent, most media outlets are tied to a target market. This is not just a vague sense of who the reader or viewer is, it is often an exact market segment, as defined by the people who sell advertising spaces and slots. (Marketers have to be able to say to potential advertisers something like: "This magazine reaches 200,000 professional female readers aged 22-35.") In order to keep those readers, the magazine must cater to them, including to their interests and values. Media outlets want to mesh with the outlook and biases of their audience and are therefore likely to bias forecast material (new or republished) toward those interests, selecting parts or framing information in a way that appeals or does not run counter to expectations.

A "quality" media outlet will be less vulnerable to this, but commercial media companies are all driven by the same basic imperative: sell more newspapers or raise the number of viewers or "eyeballs" to become more attractive to advertisers and therein more lucrative.

For better or worse, media consumers want stimulating stories, and often the more outrageous, the better. Newspapers don't fly off the newsstand if they report a balanced forecast in a sober way. The newsy spin sells better. This creates pressures in dealing with forecast material because journalists and editors have an incentive to uncritically report the radical forecast or one that fires the imagination or stirs up a polemic. As they drop caveats from the data, they also often drop the caveats in which a forecast inference is couched, or overemphasize the part of a forecast that points to extreme or polemical outcomes.

Forecasts Where Editorial Oversight Is Lacking

While media incentives can skew a forecast, lack of editorial process can create a bias-prone situation, too. In the old days, the physical and economic realities of publishing in any publicly accessible media meant that a forecast necessarily involved a number of people and a meaningful investment of resources. This didn't certify objectivity but would often balance extreme or fringe viewpoints. It was, in effect, a form of forecast filtering. With the Internet we have autonomous, often anonymous, "free" publication and editorial filters on forecast dissemination can be circumvented. Blogs, wikis, podcasts, and other social-content-sharing sites are flattening the dissemination of information.

This is very invigorating in that it offers new ways to disseminate foresight (and new ways to research it). It opens forecasting to a wider range of providers and consumers and makes better use of multimedia. But, of course, it means that anyone, or any organization can be out there in front of the world, making predictions. This is not to imply that any particular self-published forecast is unreliable, but on average such forecasts are worth less than those that have been through an editorial or peer review. The publishing function is, on the whole, the friend of the forecast consumer.

Due process may take different forms. In a newspaper it means that a news editor, copyeditor, and other editorial staff have seen the story. (But sometimes the publication process is less rigorous than it appears, particularly where famous people write articles in the general press and often nobody is allowed to touch the copy.) At a magazine, the copy has likely been both editorially reviewed and fact-checked. In an academic journal, an article will have been peer-refereed. At a reputable media outlet, analyst firm, a known entity such as a government agency, or book publisher, there are people whose job it is to make sure the data and its use is balanced and credible. They have something to lose if it is not.

The Futurist's Bias

If the forecaster is a professional futurist or someone who is in the business of trend-spotting, he or she will be subject to another strong interpretive bias—seeing change where often none exists.

> If the forecaster is a professional futurist or someone who is in the business of trend-spotting, he or she will be subject to another strong interpretive bias—seeing change where often none exists.

Futurists and forecasters soon talk themselves out of a job if they don't see big change ahead. Anticipating fundamental, rapid transition is part of the way they legitimize their existence and make their discourse relevant and attractive. To a certain extent, this is fair enough—if futurists are not going to do stretch thinking and big-picture thinking, then nobody is. And the intellectual playfulness of the field is often missed by gray-suits. But futurists clearly have an enormous vested interest in predicting big changes.

Also, people who think about the future professionally are not a representative sample of the population. With the best of intentions they are, almost without exception, people who are pro-change and pro-new ideas. Also, many work or have worked in corporate technology or R&D functions and are very up-to-date with new technology. This often biases them toward seeing rapid and pervasive change in all aspects of society, whether it exists or not, and evangelizing that change.

The Technophile Bias

Futurists aside, many people follow technology closely and think about its future in their work or just for fun. This group is served by magazines and popular technology media that trade on futuristic subject matter, and editors have an incentive to pursue "the rush of the new," hyping what is coming along. This situation creates biases in overestimating the speed, extent, and importance of technology-driven change. Every possible new development becomes "the next big thing that will change everything." In these cases, as commonly in bias situations, the cost of being wrong is low or nil, and the benefits of talking up change are significant.

Technophiles will be dazzled by the emerging technological toy box. It is likely that they are themselves early adopter gadget fans and assume the broader market is as keen and ready to try new technologies as they are. Infatuation clouds their judgment of market or political resistance. They anticipate more progress in the labs than will credibly occur, and overestimate how quickly it will be turned into products, and how quickly those products will be adopted. Market forces acting on the future are discussed more fully in Chapter 5.

Asking the Political Questions

These various bias traps guide us to the situations where biased forecasts lurk. Forecast consumers improve their understanding of genuinely likely future events by recognizing these situations and critically interacting with forecast data and interpretations that emerge from them. More broadly, forecast consumers should critically evaluate the contextual conditions of a forecast's creation, production, and dissemination, asking who produced it and what interests might they have? Where was it published? Who is it talking to? Whose interests are being served?

To take a concrete example, let's say we are faced with a piece that forecasts migration of the Internet to multiple mobile platforms and the ability, across multiple platforms, to guarantee secure communications. It may be that the forecast was put out by a civil liberties organization trying to head off government restriction of Internet technologies on national security grounds. It may be that the forecast is allied to a mobile technology research institute with an interest in defining industry standards, or another altogether different set of interests. In testing for forecast bias one could ask, What factors are motivating the discourse and causing its production? Who is it created for—who is its primary audience? Where did it first appear? Was it put out for general public consumption? Was it a military forecast? Did it appear in a specialist journal? In other words, who, primarily, is it speaking to? Why? What debate about the future does it form part of? What is it justifying? What is it lobbying for or against? What incentives apply and how will the forecast fulfill them? Whose interests are served or whose cause furthered?

But sometimes forecasts manage to shed their contextual clues, particularly when their findings are cited in the media, or in another forecast where the original publication conditions are dropped. Sometimes there are hidden sponsors of the forecast with specific agendas. Also, sometimes forecasts are very technically complex and difficult for the lay person to understand and judge effectively. In these situations, reputation of the source becomes key.

Reputation of Author and Organization

If we know the source and orientation of the forecaster or forecasting organization, credentials are a guide to forecast trustworthiness. A poor reputation is a red flag, but a good reputation is obviously no guarantee. In forecasting, as in every field, branding gives us a shortcut to quality. As we don't have the time or resources to investigate every toaster before buying one, we often don't have the time or resources to investigate every fact that comes our way, and we legitimately rely more readily on the data of organizations that have a reputation for better research and fairer forecasts.

An institution in the business of creating and disseminating data for the long term—a top research center or a government agency with a good reputation and track record—is more likely to be a balanced source. It certainly has more to lose than a fly-by-night if it is caught. Government reporting of data should be, and often is, the benchmark for good quality data. (But depending on the circumstances, this is sometimes not the case. Government agencies often have a significant vested interest in how some numbers—for example, the GNP or the unemployment rate—turn out. In reporting unemployment, for example, the definition may be subtly manipulated, excluding those choosing not to work, which can lower the headline figure.)

> Bias almost always has a history.

Bias almost always has a history. It is reassuring if an organization or publisher has a reputation for balanced forecasting built up over years. It is helpful if the forecast author or authors are associated with a known and trusted institution and have a stake in maintaining that reputation. If an author is known to take a position, or an organization known to take a certain line, chances are extremely high that this will be happening in the forecast you are presented with.

Trade and professional associations groups often produce primary industry data as well as forecasts based on this data. On the one hand, this can generally be trusted to be an agnostic pan-industry view that caters to various stakeholders. On the other, an industry group or association has a clear incentive to promote the interests of its members, particularly in talking up their relevance in the broader economy. Industry forecasts are also readily available from commercial data sources—groups such as *Gartner Inc.*, or *Forrester Research*—that research an industry area and sell data and forecasts to interested parties. Here the issue is less a biased agenda than a bias to sales. Where data and forecasts are for profit, each research day drives up "cost of goods sold," so incentives are present to drive efficiencies that may cut corners in due process.

Nonprofit and public service organizations and other special interest groups also routinely produce and disseminate numbers. Generally speaking, their record is patchy, less for manipulating numbers than for leaving out entire countering data sets and points of view: The needs of advocacy and lobbying overwhelm the need for balance. However, it is important not to make the mistake of thinking fringe organizations always have less credible data. These groups are sometimes so imbedded in an issue, or otherwise have specialist sources, such that they have data that nobody else has or is willing to share. Islamic Support DC (fictitious) could provide future thinking about attacks on Western troops in Kabul that may be better than anything put out by the Department of Defense.

Having examined problems in data reliance and biases in forecast interpretation, in the following chapter we look at problems in forecasting that come from our own cognitive and perceptual frames.

Notes

1. The relatively new "prediction markets" forecasting technique tries specifically to solve this problem by giving forecasters, or those being tapped for their forecast knowledge, real incentives for being right. In a prediction market, participants use play money to "buy" and "sell" stock in different predictions, based on what they think is likely to actually occur, but typically get real-world rewards for holding the right stock (the right prediction).
2. B. Seidensticker, *FutureHype* (San Francisco: BK Books, 2006).
3. G. Hamel and C.K. Prahalad, *Competing for the Future* (Boston: HBS Press, 1994).

CHAPTER 4

Zeitgeist and Perception: How We Can't Escape Our Own Mind

N OUR QUEST TO TRACK DOWN THE ELEMENTS OF forecast that cause them to be wrong, we have so far identified quality of factual information and quality of interpretation of those facts. We have seen that future-influencing forecasts are much more likely to create or tolerate interpretive bias in both these areas, while future-aligning forecasts will, as far as possible, seek to eliminate it. However, both kinds of forecasting are inevitably exposed to a broader form of interpretive bias that has to do with the forecaster's mental model or "paradigm," and the spirit of the times when the forecast is made. In this chapter we investigate situations where forecast failure is caused by failure to escape our mental models.

The Construction of Meaning: Why "Truth" Is Subjective

In *The Critique of Pure Reason*, Immanuel Kant argued that the human mind is an active participant in the creation of experience, not just a passive "empty vessel" recipient of knowledge. In other words, we participate in rendering knowledge, and it is not possible to transcend the bounds of our own minds to access the pure "external" truth, assuming such a thing exists. There is, in other words, no knowledge that precedes our construction of it. All knowledge is "produced" in the mind, and this filtered perception of the world is the only version accessible to us. Our knowledge is inextricably linked to our own perception and our filters.

This leap turned the world of philosophy on its head. It put human perception and experience at the heart of entire fields of study—the human sciences—and forced a revisiting of the grounds of the pure sciences. As a direct descendent of the Kantian revolution, French philosopher Michel Foucault, in *The Order of Things*, developed the concept of the "episteme," by which he means the underlying, invisible conditions of how we evaluate and order knowledge, which frame inquiry and make knowledge possible. An episteme is an *a priori* underlying system of thinking and viewing the world, which defines and orders knowledge.

Building on Gaston Bachelard's concept of "epistemic breaks" in the sciences, Foucault's insight was that epistemic conditions across the entire knowledge spectrum change from one era to the next—thus changing what counts as valid knowledge, indeed even what counts as valid questions—in relatively sudden shifts. Foucault argues that in the last 500 years, Western thought has undergone fundamental shifts in its "archeology" of knowledge, with each shift changing the underlying constitutive framework of human perception and valid basis of thought itself, leading to entirely different interpretations of the world. In Foucault's analysis of this "history of truth" we have gone from a Renaissance thought-framework based on visual and conceptual identity, to a Classical-era framework based on rationality, to a Modern framework based on humanism and constitutive perception (the Kantian revolution and birth of the human sciences).[1]

Working at Berkeley at more or less the same time, Thomas Kuhn published *The Structure of Scientific Revolutions*, in which he argued that scientific knowledge in each era is made possible by its "paradigm"—a meta-context that shapes the perceptions and assumptions of all practitioners regardless of whether they are aware of it. He argues, as Bachelard had, that evidence for the existence of these knowledge-framing paradigms is that scientific knowledge does not advance via a steady, linear, incremental accumulation of new knowledge—it undergoes revolutions. There is typically a lengthy period of quiet where well-established theories work, but they begin to creak under the weight of observations that cannot be adequately explained, until there is a revolution or "paradigm shift." Suddenly, the entire worldview collapses and is rebuilt to account for the nonconforming data. When the Ptolemaic universe suddenly collapsed and gave way to the Copernican, that was a paradigm shift, as was Einstein's overturning of Newtonian physics. The germ theory of disease was a paradigm shift, as was the theory of plate tectonics to explain continental drift and other geological changes.

Kuhn's paradigm is narrower than Foucault's episteme, but the idea of sudden and fundamental transition is very similar. A previous set of agreements about how perceptions are to be organized and data or problems are to be understood, and even what counts as a valid form of inquiry, gives way to a new set. Suddenly, what was previously "known" is perceived as partially or entirely false. As Kuhn points out, paradigms cannot be avoided and are indeed essential to thought, saying: "No natural history can be interpreted in the absence of at least some implicit body of intertwined theoretical and methodological belief that permits selection, evaluation, and criticism."[2] But as paradigms produce thought, they also filter out what doesn't fit or cannot be accounted for. During periods of "normal science"—between revolutions—it is apparent that scientists ignore findings that do not conform to the current paradigm and very often entirely miss, that is, do not even "see" nonconforming data. This is "paradigm blindness," sometimes also known as "paradigm paralysis."

How Our Brains Filter Information

Experiments in the way the mind perceives, omits or misperceives, and otherwise functions to produce knowledge is the subject of many studies in cognitive psychology and brain research. In a 2005 *Scientific American* article, "How Blind Are We?" researchers at the Center for Brain and Cognition at the University of California, San Diego, report on the now-famous gorilla experiment.[3] Participants were shown a video of a basketball game and asked to count the number of passes through a short but frenetic period. The researchers had someone dressed in a gorilla suit cross the floor, walk among the players, turn to face the viewers and thump his chest before leaving. Fifty percent of people failed to notice the gorilla. There are many such studies—where subjects are partially distracted and seemingly obvious changes not noticed—demonstrating our "inattentional blindness" and proving that our eyes are not "video cameras" that make a faithful recording of the world. This blindness is essential to thought—we must filter experience in order not to be overwhelmed by the mass and jumble of sensory inputs.

But the cost is that things that do not fit with the situation, or that appear irrelevant to a current task (particularly when the brain is overloaded), are filtered out, and therefore we miss or misrecognize unexpected events.

The ordering and filtering function that we bring to information is most easily and popularly seen in figure-ground studies, where two (or sometimes more) images can be seen in a particular drawing depending how the observer looks. Well-known examples of figure-ground studies are "the vase versus two faces," or "old hag versus busty young lady." It is very often the case that, in more complex figure-ground studies, some people cannot see both images no matter how hard they try. The mental structures we create to cognitively process the world ultimately constrain us from going beyond the frames of our approach.

> The learned cognitive framework that orders our perception is constantly updated, but also goes right back to the earliest phases of our socialization and entry into language, where we learned to view and interpret the world filtered by the knowledge-organizing theories and biases of our family, community, and society.

The way our brain filters information and constructs meaning leans heavily on systems of organizing knowledge that have made sense in the past. The learned cognitive framework that orders our perception is constantly updated, but also goes right back to the earliest phases of our socialization and entry into language, where we learned to view and interpret the world filtered by the knowledge-organizing theories and biases of our family, community, and society. This "baggage" both allows us to screen and evaluate information in order to produce thought, and it also filters and blocks our vision. We struggle to see a situation afresh because we can't get past the way we currently assemble the information. The benefits of shaking off what we already know, and how we know it, are what is sought after, for example, in the Buddhist concept of "beginner's mind," or the Japanese "Sunao" (untrapped mind).

That it is very difficult to see what we have not seen before, or what lies outside our perceptive framework, was brought home by the events of 9/11. By all accounts there had been enough information—enough clues in the preceding months and years—for analysts to be able to deduce what was being planned. The evidence was all duly gathered and processed by the authorities, but the total picture did not emerge. How could the analysts processing the data have missed what was apparently staring them in the face? This was not a failure of scanning systems, nor a failure of motivation, nor intelligence, it was a failure of perception, that is, a paradigm failure.

As scientists put it, we need a "search image" for what we are looking for, and if we don't have that image, we won't recognize a new constellation of reality, even if we're looking straight at it. The planned events of 9/11 were new enough and extreme enough to lie outside of the U.S. authorities' perceptive framework, beyond then-current search images. It is telling that, not only were the national security authorities unable to see the event, but even a meeting of expert futurists in 1996, called specifically to consider world-changing "wildcard" events, was unable to see it. Delegates at the meeting enumerated hundreds of possibilities, including global wars, new religions, "superbugs," market collapse, earthquakes, and so forth, but missed anything like the events of 9/11.[4]

For the same reasons and in the same way, business decision makers are vulnerable to paradigm shifts. Almost all great failures—including great companies that hit the wall and collapse—are due to failing to see the demands of a new environment, or the capabilities of new technologies, because of paradigm blinkers. Overcoming paradigm blindness is, by contrast, often behind success in innovation. While everybody is missing the opportunity that is right in front of their nose, someone, like Fedex-creator Fred Smith, sees and grabs it. Everyone else is left thinking: "I wish I'd thought of that!"

Judgmental Heuristics: Biases in How We Think

Cognitive psychologists Tversky and Kahneman took the idea of productive, constitutive perception in another direction to investigate perceptual and judgmental heuristics and the decision-making biases in human judgment they produce. Decision heuristics are "hard-wired" proclivities or aversions by which people make judgments or take decisions when faced with complex problems or incomplete information. These heuristics work well in many circumstances, but in certain cases lead to systematic cognitive biases. The most famous heuristic bias they identified is "loss aversion"—the human tendency to prefer avoiding losses over acquiring gains. Their experiments showed that, for example, when given a choice between getting a certain $100 or having a 50% chance of getting $250 most choose the no-risk $100. However, when given the choice of a certain loss of $100 versus a 50% chance of losing $250, most were willing to gamble in an attempt to avoid losing any money.[5]

> Decision heuristics are "hard-wired" proclivities or aversions by which people make judgments or take decisions when faced with complex problems or incomplete information.

Other common human and social cognitive biases are:

- Observer-expectancy effect: Occurs when someone expects a result and unconsciously misinterprets information or manipulates an experiment or in order to find it. Observers notice behavior they expect to find and fail to notice behavior they do not expect.

- Confirmation bias: The tendency to search for or interpret information in a way that confirms one's preconceptions or to engage in behavior that elicits outcomes that confirm pre-existing beliefs.
- Herd bias, bandwagon effect, or "groupthink": The tendency to believe or do things because many other people are doing or appear to be doing them.
- Anchoring: The tendency to allow one's thinking to be swayed by an "anchor," which may or not be a fair marker. Anchoring is popularly recognized in negotiation strategy, where a high or low strategic pre-bid is made (the marker) in order to sway the perception of what is actually a fair offer.
- Recency effect: The tendency to weigh recent events more than events further in the past.
- Situational bias: Where current conditions frame what people see and how they interpret events. In a depression, for example, it is difficult to see any source of upturn. In boom times it is hard to see the crash.
- Personal validation fallacy, or "the Barnum Effect": Named in honor of the circus showman P.T. Barnum (of Barnum & Bailey Circuses), who coined the show biz philosophy: "Have a little something in it for everyone." The Barnum effect is the basis of, for example, astrological forecasts, where statements are vague enough to allow anyone and everyone can see personal validity in them. This is also known as the Forer Effect, particularly applied to believability of psychometric tests that supposedly singularly and accurately describe the test-taker's personality, but in fact are vague enough to apply to many people.
- Seeing patterns in chance events: As humans, we are often not comfortable with random causes and therefore bend over backwards to find a pattern in the data or attribute meaning

to chance events, as for example in ascribing economic reason to small market moves that are merely random.[6]

These biases are the key ones among hundreds of human-perception biases that people bring to the world. They are part of (and evidence of) perception being active and constituent in our understanding of the world, and therefore of the future. We can chip away at our cognitive biases and heuristics, particularly by questioning our assumptions, as detailed below. And a better understanding of these cognitive errors at work, and the biases they create, would no doubt improve our judgment in situations of uncertainty. However, there will never be perception without perceptual frameworks and their biases. No matter how astutely we look and how consciously we try to eliminate them, our perception biases exist. Similarly, the forecasters we are reading are perceiving the world and the future through their cognitive filters.

As an aside, this is the reason the ever-popular SWOT analysis fails as a way of thinking about (or forecasting) the future. A SWOT calls for the analyst to identify an organization's Strengths, Weaknesses, Opportunities, and Threats. But, of course, the resulting lists are paradigm-bound. Strengths or weaknesses assume what is a strength or weakness at present, for the present paradigm, for the present industry or product or nature of competition. The opportunities and threats that are perceivable to the analyst, are by definition only those obvious within current perceptions. A SWOT analysis codifies the standard view, aka "the official future," but does not prepare decision-makers for outcomes outside of this.

The Zeitgeist Bias:
Seeing Reality Through the Lens of Our Times

All of the biases listed above are at work in human thought, and must be expected in forecasting. "Zeitgeist bias," a particular form of situational bias, is very common and deserves some particular attention. *Zeitgeist,* German for "spirit of the times," refers to the full and often unconscious spectrum of intellectual views, analytical approaches, political and social concerns, and so on, that people in any era share. Evidence from the history of predicting the future shows that forecasters have been very heavily biased by the current conditions, current issues, and current state of the world at the time the forecast was made, that is by the zeitgeist. The key marker of this effect at work is when many forecasts are not only wrong, but are wrong in the same way.

> Evidence from the history of predicting the future shows that forecasters have been very heavily biased by the current conditions, current issues, and current state of the world at the time the forecast was made, that is by the zeitgeist.

Unique insight into the role zeitgeist plays in framing forecasts can be found in *Today Then: America's Best Minds Look 100 Years into the Future on the Occasion of the 1893 World's Columbian Exposition,* a collection of forecasts made at the Chicago's World Fair, and republished 100 years later.[7] While a few forecasters adequately saw technology and social outcomes, for example, "A Train Running at 100 Miles an Hour," and "The Wonderful Development of Florida," the predictions are mostly way off base. Chicago experts and notables of the day—the people invited to forecast—were steeped in the perceptions of a Midwest pioneer city, based on agriculture and agricultural trade, and these are the elements that dominate the forecasts for 1993. Europe and European ways of doing things were expected to remain a serious reference point for the U.S. economy, in a way that is unimaginable now. Strong elements of unionism, labor politics, and anarchism were foreseen—a paradigmatic concern of those times, but not ours.

Nobody would expect a 100-year forecast to be accurate, and some turn out to be more accurate than others, but what is instructive is that the fifty-plus forecasters are all handicapped in the same way—by the difficulty in seeing beyond the issues and preoccupations of nineteenth-century fin-de-siècle America. The authors singularly fail to capture the zeitgeist of 100 years later—the global, information-driven economy of the late twentieth century—which would have created a better forecast in principle even if some of the details were wrong.

The zeitgeist bias in forecasting has perhaps never been clearer than in forecast from the 1950s and 1960s, when predictions of nuclear-powered planes, vacations on Mars, eradication of disease, "too much" leisure time, and others, were common. These were wrong in the same way because of an overoptimistic reading of technology progress and an assumption of available resources and energy to fulfill any progress fantasy. In other words, they were deeply evocative of the zeitgeist: The United States had emerged from World War II as the world's superpower. The economy was booming, jobs were plentiful, higher education and research were expanding exponentially, the space race was in full swing, and there was an expectation of growing human control of nature, and unlimited resources and possibilities driven by "American ingenuity."

In these golden years of economic and technological progress, bigger and better technology bonanzas and automated conveniences were what was "in the air," and therefore routinely forecast. For example, one mid-1960s agricultural forecast envisioned indoor weather-controlled farms, robotic tractors, irrigation with desalinated seawater, and synthetic meats—singing the zeitgeist.[8] The forecast missed the real future turning points in agriculture: containerization, low commodity prices, international protectionism, agricultural biotechnologies and resistance to them, and demand for "organic" produce.

By the early 1970s the lenses with which forecasters viewed the world had changed sharply. The failure in Vietnam was becoming apparent, and unemployment and inflation were both up sharply, partly as a result of the OPEC oil embargos after 1973 that resulted in unprecedented and alarming lines at gas stations. Global financial crises, particularly in Latin America, and rapid population growth in the developing world were other dark clouds. Not surprisingly, the future views from this era changed tone dramatically. The signature forecast of the decade was the Club of Rome's "Limits to Growth" study (1972), which used long-term modeling to examine the consequences of rapid population growth, particularly in Asia and Africa, measured against finite resources, including oil. The zeitgeist had shifted, and forecasting followed suit, becoming generally far more sober and concerned with limits. Even techno-optimists, while arguing against the "doom-mongers," drastically toned down their own predictions.

After 1989, the fall of Soviet Union and the end of the Cold War provoked new thinking about global interaction and growth, and this new thinking, combined with the rise of digital technologies, the Internet, WTO agreements, and the dot.com market boom, fueled a new zeitgeist of optimism. Almost as if the previous era had not existed, suddenly people believed (and forecast) that information and communication technologies and new business models were about to solve every human problem, from creating global digital universities to preventive dental scanning. In 1999, a widely respected corporate futurist, Peter Schwartz, was drawn to coauthor a book called *The Long Boom,* anticipating twenty-five years of unprecedented U.S.-led global prosperity, international peace and harmony, rising standards of living, enhanced personal freedoms, and a better environment.[9]

By the end of 2001, the NASDAQ bubble had burst, Al-Qaeda had struck buildings that symbolized U.S. power, the "War on Terror" had begun, and the entire rosy 1990s and all the forecasts that went with it, were finished. Enter the current zeitgeist. Forecasts made in the early twenty-first century offer a generally more circumspect outlook in the face of a more dangerous, politically fragmented world, the rise of social conservatism, and the stark erosion of civil liberties. Other major strands that frame the current era are global warming, globalization, and the economic emergence of China.

Forecasts from this base are undoubtedly subject to these framing perceptions. We assume these will be the issues of the future, but the lessons of zeitgeist bias suggest that entirely other issues will dominate the agenda in decades to come. As surely as night follows day, the times will turn and a new era will dawn, with new issues, situations, and relationships we cannot see yet structuring the world. (It is not that new political threats or global warming or China's emergence will go away, just that they will be factored in—people will be used to them, adjustments will have been made, and they will no longer be the dominant new thing pressing on the collective mind.) Forecasters who assume our current issues, priorities, and concerns of today will be those of the future will turn out to have made poor forecasts.

Consensus and Expert Forecasts May Be Paradigm-Bound

Consensus forecasts are especially vulnerable to paradigm or zeitgeist bias. Forecasts are often legitimized by saying the predictions made are "the consensus of many opinions." If many people agree, this is usually worth more than a lone voice, but the situational-zeitgeist bias casts doubt on all consensus-based and consensus-legitimized forecasting because the consensus around the forecast may be merely the zeitgeist effect.

> *If many people agree, this is usually worth more than a lone voice, but the situational-zeitgeist bias casts doubt on all consensus-based and consensus-legitimized forecasting because the consensus around the forecast may be merely the zeitgeist effect.*

The most popular consensus-based forecasting process is the Delphi method, in which interviewees (often experts in their field) are asked to assess the likelihood and timing of predicted events put before them. Through iterative rounds of questions, where each member separately responds, the range of likely future events and the timing of their emergence is narrowed until a consensus position is reached. The technique does elicit the common viewpoint among the group, but does not guarantee that the interviewees are not all wrong in the same way.

Forecasts are also often legitimized by showing that they are the opinions of an expert or experts in the field. The qualifications of these individuals or expert panels are trumpeted to impress us as to the value of the forecast—and we allow ourselves to be guided by their credentials and authority, particularly in areas where we ourselves know relatively little. (We are also often swayed by success and weigh the words of successful people more highly. If Warren Buffet has something to say about the future of any topic, not necessarily investments and securities, people will pay attention.) On one hand, this is fair enough: Experts have the obvious advantage of inside and specialist knowledge, contacts, and experience, and should therefore have a more authoritative base than the lay person from which to see changes and future outcomes in their fields. If they cannot tell us what is coming next in their area of expertise, who can?

But experts are as likely as anyone to be bound by the current paradigm and may be the last people to be able to see beyond it, never more so than in areas undergoing rapid or complex change.

They typically know so much about the old way of doing things that they are likely the last to see new possibilities. Futurist Edie Weiner calls this problem "educated incapacity"—the incapacity of knowing too much about present systems and solutions to be able to see outside of them.[10] So a doctor may know a lot about healthcare, but nothing about the forces of change affecting it. A civil servant may know how her department works, but have little concept of the future of government. This expertise is about the present, not the future, and may stop them seeing the future.

As experts are often industry or company insiders, there is usually an overlap between expert paradigm paralysis and "insider bias" (see previous chapter). In fact, experts often use their expert experience and insider status to pooh-pooh external change and reinforce a paradigm bias, saying "it could never work" or "that's not the way things get done around here." *Encyclopedia Britannica's* management was saying that about free content and digital media storage in the 1990s, as the company went swiftly to the wall.

Challenging Our Mental Model: Questioning Assumptions

> Our cognitive framework, which circumscribes and orders our perceptions, shapes how we view events and also prevents us from seeing things we are not expecting or have not seen before.

In summary, it is clear that we all participate in constructing knowledge from the stimuli around us, and this construction is subject to considerable individual and group-based paradigms, including organizing information according to the current zeitgeist. Our cognitive framework, which circumscribes and orders our perceptions, shapes how we view events and also prevents us from seeing things we are not expecting or have not seen before. We miss crucial items or incorrectly weight factors that influence the future, which prevents us from making good forecasts.

As Louis Pasteur said, "chance favors the prepared mind," and the holy grail is clearly to find a way to prepare our minds: to expand our frames and see patterns in a new way or from alternate points of view, in order to be able to overcome or at least mitigate cognitive filters. There is no simple answer to overcoming our perceptual frames. Even if it was possible to overcome our own cognitive framework—to, as it were, give our paradigm the slip—it is by definition impossible to know whether we have succeeded. However, there is one simple technique by which the savvy forecast consumer can investigate and challenge the mental model implied in a forecast. This is by identifying and questioning the assumptions on which it is based.

Every forecast is necessarily based on one or more assumptions about what present factors or forces are important and how they will change, come together, and resolve to arrive at a future situation. The assumption is the means by which the forecaster "casts forward" from present observation to future outcome. For example, the current common forecast that says China will have the largest economy in the world by 2030, assumes continuance of the current rate of growth in the Chinese economy. It also assumes current levels of inequality in growth rates between China and the United States (currently the world's largest national economy); Chinese access to natural resources; a growing Chinese skills base; and the lack of destabilizing conditions such as war or terror, etc. A growing skills base in turn assumes a commitment to education and training. Access to natural resources assumes the diplomatic ability to source materials and the eco-

> *A forecast is only as good as the assumptions it rests on, and the better the assumptions, the better the forecast will be.*

nomic ability to pay for them. In short, the forward casting is based on many assumptions, which are themselves based on other assumptions. A forecast is only as good as the assumptions it rests on, and the better the assumptions, the better the forecast will be.

The question then becomes, how valid are these assumptions? If they are good assumptions, the forecast will be close to the mark. If the assumptions are poor—if, for example, access to raw materials is constrained or investment in education lags—the forecast will veer dramatically off course. In fact, experience shows that a forecast based on poor assumptions will not be out by inches, it will be out by miles. For example, the failed 1990s forecast of the emergence of the "paperless office" made a host of interlocking assumptions: rapid evolution of digital technology, ease of use being equal or better than paper systems, cost being equal or lower than current systems, improved software security, market readiness and user adoption, and so on. These were poor assumptions.

A forecast's assumptions may be good or bad at the time the forecast was made. But, over time, all assumptions deteriorate. For example, it may have been valid to assume in the 1970s that immigrants would quickly acculturate and integrate into their new country. Now, with virtually free telephony, more frequent and cheaper air travel, and Internet-based cultural resources, this assumption may be less valid. In a fast-moving field or industry, assumptions date faster. So even where an assumption accurately represents a link between the present and the future, the world will change over time, and this link becomes progressively or suddenly invalid. Therefore, the longer the forecast view, the more likely assumptions will be poor by the end of the time horizon it deals with. As we will see in the chapters ahead, trend-extrapolation and quantitative forecasting are valid approaches, while assumptions hold, that is, for short and some short-medium horizons. Beyond this, extrapolations based on current assumptions will give wildly wrong answers every time, no matter how fancy the extrapolative method or how powerful the computer that crunches the numbers.

Identifying and Testing Assumptions

Assumptions made by forecasters are based on their underlying beliefs—the mental model or paradigm they are working from. While it is difficult to identify the cognitive framework of any forecast or forecaster for the same reasons it is difficult to identify our own, it is reasonably simple to question the assumptions that support it. If we "reverse engineer" the forecast to identify its assumptions, test their validity, consider alternative assumptions, and see how these lead to alternative inferences about the future, we can escape the forecaster's cognitive and paradigm biases.

Testing assumptions involves the following steps:

- **Extract the assumptions.** Sometimes a forecast's assumptions will be explicit. The author will say, for example, "I am assuming that the minimum wage is going to stay at present levels," or "I assume the political will to pursue biometric testing will be in place." But more often the assumptions are tacit and the savvy reader will have to impute them. All we need to do is ask, "What must the forecast be assuming in order to get from the present to the anticipated future state?"

    The task of extracting assumptions also includes identifying missing (usually negative) assumptions. In other words, asking, "What assumptions need to be made to arrive at this forecast, but are missing?" Often an overoptimistic forecast will proceed merrily to the future by failing to make the necessary negative assumptions—assumptions of constraints or brakes on the emergence of a forecast, failing to adequately explore negative downstream effects that prevent a future emerging or slow it down.

✧ **Test and reverse the assumptions.** Eliciting the assumptions immediately invites us to think: How good are they? And what would happen if an assumption was reversed, or if we were to make an alternative assumption? For example, we may come across a forecast that says: "Eighty percent of the world will live in cities by 2025," and be able to deduce that the forecast must be assuming continued urban migration, probably based on cities continuing to be the center of professional work and prosperity. We may however question and reverse this assumption, arguing that information and communications technology and rapid improvement in virtual reality will allow people to be able to work from distant locations and that cities may be depleted of the best and brightest in favor of smaller towns with higher standards of living.

In this way, questioning, exploring, and reversing assumptions challenges and improves a forecast. Creating alternative future projections by reversing key assumptions is the basis of the scenario forecasting method discussed in Chapter 9.

Notes

1. M. Foucault, *The Order of Things* (London: Routledge, 1966); and *The Archeology of Knowledge* (London: Tavistock, 1969).
2. T. Kuhn, *The Structure of Scientific Revolutions* (Chicago: University of Chicago Press, 1962).
3. V. Ramachandran, "How Blind Are We?" citing a study by D. Simons and C. Chabris. Retrieved January 2007 from ScientificAmerican.com (May 18, 2005).

4. K. Fulton, & E. Eidinow, "Wild Cards," GBN, 1996. Retrieved April 2007 from www.gbn.org
5. D. Kahneman, P. Slovic, and A.Tversky (Eds.), *Judgment under Uncertainty: Heuristics and Biases* (Cambridge, UK: Cambridge University Press, 1982).
6. See N. Taleb, *Fooled by Randomness: The Hidden Role of Chance in Life and in the Markets* (New York: Random House, 2005).
7. D. Walter (Ed.), *Today Then: America's Best Minds Look 100 Years into the Future on the Occasion of the 1893 World's Columbian Exposition* (Helena, MT: American World Geographic Publishing, 1992). In 1893, for the World's Columbian Exposition in Chicago, the American Press Association assembled a collection of forecasts for the year 1993. The best, brightest, and most prominent minds of the day—engineers, writers, politicians, poets, and industrialists—were asked to look forward 100 years among them.
8. Cited in S. Schaars, *Megamistakes* (New York: Free Press, 1989).
9. P. Schwartz et al., *The Long Boom* (New York: Perseus Books, 1999).
10. E. Weiner and A. Brown, *Futurethink* (Upper Saddle River, NJ: Pearson-Prentice Hall, 2006).

CHAPTER 5

The Power of User Utility: How Consumers Drive and Block Change

N THE PREVIOUS CHAPTER WE HIGHLIGHTED PROB-
lems in forecast information and interpretation that enable us to identify poor forecasts. In this chapter we move to consider economic and market forces, and the role of consumers, in promoting or resisting the future. In Chapter 6 we consider other drivers and blockers of change and how viewing these dynamics improves our forecast filtering.

"Our Future in Space"

The forecasts that surrounded the future of space travel and exploration are perhaps the most high-profile and comprehensively poor set of forecasts ever made, and therefore provide a good vantage point to consider what can go wrong in forecasting. From the 1950s, space was a huge topic of interest. All significant earthbound exploration challenges had been overcome, technology was moving rapidly, and what lay ahead, unconquered, was space. The need to explore it was deeply in the zeitgeist. At the same time, the Cold War created the specific situation where beating the Soviets in prestige projects was an important priority, important enough to divert massive resources to it. J.F. Kennedy's rousing (future-influencing) 1961 prediction of putting a man on the moon by the end of the decade motivated and galvanized the United States, and the resulting Gemini and Apollo programs made this not only a human achievement but a successful prediction.[1] As a result, analysts of all stripes were quick to project the trend and predict a moon base, lunar communities by 2000, followed soon by trips to Mars and beyond, and on to the limits of space. . . .

The last man to set foot on the moon was in 1973. The Space Shuttle tried to maintain forward momentum under the guise of scientific research, not without disaster, and an almost inconsequential international space station has been built. To this day there are many who cry into their soup over the lack of space exploration and conquest. So what happened? The groundswell of prediction was wrong because it failed to see that putting a few U.S. men into orbit did not add enough value to enough peoples' lives to justify the expense—particularly in the economically uncertain 1970s. In the end, the majority of consumers voted with their wallets to postpone, if not entirely eviscerate, human space exploration.

The Role of Consumer Power in Creating the Future

To understand the role of consumers and the market in creating and responding to change, we need to go back to some economic fundamentals. Economics is constructed around scarcity: how humans attempt to satisfy unlimited wants with scarce or limited resources.

> Total utility is the sum of all benefits a consumer gains from consuming particular goods or services, minus the costs involved.

Overcoming scarcity demands the efficient use of resources—that is, a "rational person" will attempt to minimize the limits on wants through best use of resources. The economic term for the benefit a consumer gets from a good or service is "utility." Total utility is the sum of all benefits a consumer gains from consuming particular goods or services, minus the costs involved. Economics reasonably assumes that consumers will act in their own (or group or community or national) self-interest in order to maximize their total utility.

Maximizing utility could imply, for example, finding the same product at two different prices and buying where it is cheaper, or switching allegiance to a new solution that offers what one currently gets, but at a cheaper price. But it can also mean *spending more* to get a higher quality item—if the gain in quality outweighs the gain in price. Clearly, sticker price is a component of utility, but a utility analysis does not say the cheapest solution rules. To use a simple example, most consumers may be happy to pay $10 for an ordinary umbrella to achieve (the utility of) staying dry in the rain. Most would not pay $5 for a low-grade umbrella because they would know it would break after several uses. Even though it is cheaper, its total utility is lower. They would also not pay $40 for a superior-quality brand-name umbrella because they would figure they will be just as dry with a standard umbrella. The gain is not worth the cost for most people—their total utility would not go up. When caught in a downpour without an umbrella, consumers may pay a street seller $5 for a low-grade umbrella they would otherwise not buy, because they are factoring in the benefit of not getting soaked right now. That is, in a downpour the utility gain offered by the low-grade umbrella includes not getting wet right now, and the total utility is worth $5 to many people.

So it is important not to confuse a utility analysis with a price analysis. Total utility looks at the whole picture of costs and benefits and anticipates that users also consider "non-economic factors" such as environmental impact, moral implications, safety, public benefit, image and fashion, local or national prestige, convenience and ease of use (time cost), and so on, as part of their cost-benefit calculation in determining their overall best interest. One example is how child car seats, bicycle helmets, and smoke alarms have been adopted in most developed societies, despite their extra cost. The benefit of disaster avoidance outweighs the extra cost for most people, therein utility is raised, and therefore these products became part of our lives. Similarly, with testing of cosmetics on animals or buying sweatshop sneakers—many people would rather pay more than have this happen. Their utility calculation includes placing a value on ethical and humanitarian practices. This also explains how governments, NGOs, or similar organizations are able to get people to do things that go counter to a strict price calculation of benefit. If a lobby group encourages the population to "buy Brazilian and save Brazilian jobs," it is asking the public to avoid the easy economic win of a cheaper item for the long-term national benefit. It is saying: "Even though the immediate price may be higher—that is, immediate utility lower—in the long run the total utility of all for us will be higher."

Following this thinking, to judge whether any innovation has a chance to succeed and become part of the future, one must ask, Will the innovation offer a greater jump in total user benefits than jump in total costs, that is, will there be a net utility gain? Rational consumers will inevitably judge alternative options against the current way they do things and won't make a change in their consumption patterns unless it raises their utility. In the economic jargon, consumers are "indifferent" to any bundle of goods that represent the same level of utility to them. They will not be indifferent when choosing between a higher and lower utility bundle.

Marginal Utility and Diminishing Marginal Returns

In economics a "marginal" cost or benefit refers to the difference made by one extra unit added to a total—the specific cost or benefit of the extra unit. So the marginal cost of labor is the cost of adding one more worker. The marginal tax rate is the rate of tax on each extra dollar earned. Marginal utility, therefore, is the additional utility a consumer gains from consuming one more unit of a good or service.

> Marginal utility, therefore, is the additional utility a consumer gains from consuming one more unit of a good or service.

The "law of diminishing returns" holds that a consumer will get less utility *per unit* for each extra unit consumed. While her total utility goes up (more is consumed), her marginal utility for each additional unit goes down. For example, if a person has not had anything to eat for days, a first bowl of pasta put in front of him has a very high utility—survival. The second bowl would too, but may not be critical to sustaining life and health. By the third bowl the consumer will be slowing down, and when offered a fourth, he would probably not be able to eat it all—that is, he won't get any benefit from it. With each additional unit, the consumer experiences less utility. Similarly, if a consumer has access to one television channel, then adding one more channel represents a great leap in utility, but if he has 500 channels, adding one more will not even be noticed.

Sometimes utility may diminish gradually. In other cases, it may reach a "tipping point" (hey, I'm full!) and diminish rapidly after that. Either way, there comes a point where a consumer either cannot detect or cannot use the extra benefit offered. The cost of the extra unit of value, however, remains—the cost of making the first bowl of pasta and the fourth bowl is the same. (Production costs may go down slightly due to economies of scale, but it also may go up due to limits of technology—see below). Therefore, on average, costs continue to rise as the benefit tails off. This leads us inexorably to the point where there is no net utility gain, and thereafter, utility loss. Or, put another way, the cost/benefit of the next marginal unit is negative. That unit will therefore never exist. It will not be part of the future. The fourth bowl of pasta is not made.

A demonstration of the law of diminishing marginal returns—and therefore diminishing net utility—and its effect of what occurs in the world, can be seen in the history of tall buildings. New technologies in steel construction allowed buildings to be built to greater heights from the end of the nineteenth century. The nine-story Home Insurance Building in Chicago, the first to use steel frame construction, became known as the first "skyscraper" in 1885.[2] As other the technical barriers were overcome, including safe, electrified elevators and water pumps, building height rose rapidly. The Metropolitan Life Insurance Tower (1909, 50 stories) was followed by the Woolworth Building (1913, 60 stories); the Chrysler Building (1930, 77 stories); and the Empire State Building (1931,102 stories).[3] But, that is where the acceleration in building height ended. Some incremental height records have since been achieved—for example by the Petronas Towers, Kuala Lumpur; and Taipei 101, Taiwan—but the sharp growth trend to taller and taller buildings ended over seventy-five years ago.

The benefit of each extra story for a building developer is the additional rental space acquired. So why not go higher? Architects and engineers could no doubt *technically* build a 200-story building, and probably achieve even a 500-story building if there was call for it. But building heights stopped increasing because each added story raises practical and operational problems. The cost, difficulty, and danger of construction and maintenance increases. The problems of servicing the building, including moving people in and out en masse, increases. The danger of fire, earthquake and, famously, terrorism also increases. There comes a point where the total (economic and non-economic) cost outweighs the benefits—that is, the net additional utility of each additional story to consumers becomes negative. Investment, and therefore building, stops at this cost/benefit balance.[4]

The history of passenger air travel speed offers us another example. Passenger air travel speed saw a steady upward curve from the Wright Brothers' first flight at 10 miles an hour to propeller travel at about 180 mph. In 1952 the *British Overseas Aircraft Corporation (BOAC)* introduced the first commercial jet-powered airliner between London and Johannesburg, raising the average speed of air travel to 480 mph. From there commercial travel speed increased slowly to the introduction of the Boeing 747, with a cruising speed of 560 mph in 1970.

In 1976 the Anglo-French Concorde was introduced into commercial service, flying at 1,335 mph. Industry experts predicted were that there would be 400 Concordes in service by 1989. But here is where the utility of speed started to tail off, and the Concorde turned out to be a rarefied, expensive service, not the future of commercial air travel at all. Only fourteen ever flew commercially and the Concorde was decommissioned in 2003 after many loss-making years (not primarily because of an accident at Charles de Gaulle airport—many other planes have had accidents without causing the model to be mothballed). It turns out that the speed commercial airliners have flown since 1970 is in fact the optimal speed for consumers when all costs and benefits are factored in. It is the point where the benefit of speed balances with costs, including fuel cost, safety costs, and environmental and noise pollution considerations. Going faster would create price rises (fewer seats available; more fuel required), and the time saved is not worth the price hike for most consumers. Adding more speed adds less utility than cutting ticket prices or adding safety features, thus we reached the effective speed limit of commercial aviation.

There is absolutely no indication that airliners will be made to go faster anytime soon, even though technologically we could very easily do it. The foreseeable future of commercial airplanes can be seen in the Airbus A380, launched in 2007, which flies at 560 mph, the same speed as commercial jets were flying in 1970.[5]

This is not to say that, eventually, new technologies will not cause another jump in commercial air travel speed. They may do so. But this will happen only when total utility is raised by doing it. The test these prospective new aviation technologies will have to pass is not just the ability to provide speed, it is the ability to go faster without raising ticket prices, or environmental impact, or compromising safety, that is, without lowering total utility.[6]

The Role of Consumer Utility in Advancing or Denying Change

The history of commercial airline travel is a deeply instructive example in forecasting. Speaking about commercial aviation in 1972, then U.S. Vice President Spiro Agnew said, "It must be obvious to anyone with any sense of history and any awareness of human nature that there will be SSTs (supersonic transport). And Super SSTs. And Super-Super SSTs. Mankind is simply not going to sit back with the Boeing 747 and say 'This is as far as we go'."[7]

This was a very poor prediction indeed. In fact, the future of commercial air travel lay almost entirely in the *opposite* direction to that which Agnew forecast in 1972: not faster but cheaper (budget air travel), safer, and more environmentally friendly. In other words, the future was not determined by technology "wows" nor by human ambition, but by what, for most people, represented a real if prosaic gain in utility. Unfortunately, Agnew was not making a unique mistake. He was making the most common mistake in forecasting—being so infatuated with new technologies that he forgot to consider the cost-benefit equation. Interestingly, right about this time an entrepreneur named Herb Kelleher, founder of *Southwest Airlines*, made a prediction of his own: that raising utility in the airline industry, at that time, was to be found in cutting costs to users. Prior to Southwest, flying was a relatively elite, expensive form of transport. Southwest took its first flight in 1971 and has been profitable every year since 1973. The Concorde never made a cent for the BA/Air France consortium. It is no surprise that Southwest became "the future" in the airline industry, spawning many no-frills look-alikes in the United States and across the world. Nobody copied the Concorde.

> Often a new product or service it is adopted despite a price rise—where additional benefit outweighs additional cost.

As mentioned, a utility analysis is not a simple price or cost analysis, so cost-cutting is not always the route to the future. Often a new product or service it is adopted despite a price rise—where additional benefit outweighs additional cost. *Cirque de Soleil* dramatically raised the price of circus tickets, creating $100-a-ticket performances that still sell out around the world night after night, because of the new benefits it added to the circus shows.

From Technology-Push to Market-Pull

Forecasters who view the world from technology-driven perspectives often do fabulous and detailed work in figuring out how technology is evolving. While there is no question that technology change is a major force behind much change, spotting emerging technologies and imagining humans using them brings analysts no closer to seeing the future, and very often takes them in the wrong direction. It makes them merely the "Spiro Agnew" of their fields.

> While there is no question that technology change is a major force behind much change, spotting emerging technologies and imagining humans using them brings analysts no closer to seeing the future, and very often takes them in the wrong direction.

But techno-fantasizing is a very common way of thinking about the future. The result is a long history of embarrassing techno-forecasting mis-hits. A paradigmatic example is the 1960s study by the Insurance Information Institute entitled "A Report on Tomorrow," published by *National Underwriter*, projecting what life would be like in the 1980s. It predicted automated highways, orbiting factories in space, undersea hotels, and ready-made houses delivered by helicopter."[8] At the same time, other research reports anticipated moving sidewalks, manned moon bases, 3D television, space tourism, solar-powered cars, night-sky advertising, nuclear-powered aircraft, household robo-maids, quadraphonic stereo, and microwave telephony. These predictions were published in credible journals and news magazines. While they were, from a technology perspective, perfectly possible, a tiny fraction of what was predicted actually emerged because general utility gain for most people was absent. (The technology-inspired "killer app" of the early 1980s, the Walkman—providing huge new user utility by making stereo music portable—was not predicted.)

Lest we think these errors are all in the past, it is worth considering some current examples. It has been widely forecast that we are soon going to be living in "smart" homes with central infosystems that automate home security, lighting, appliances, heating and cooling, audio and video systems, and so on. Smart systems will feed your pet when you're gone, enable you to turn lights on and off remotely, heat the property before you arrive, start coffee in the morning before you awake, automatically order milk and other groceries when you run low, and so on. Sure, the technologies for these systems are easily and widely available. However, this prediction does not pass the utility test. It is a wrong prediction for any period other than the long term, no matter who did the analysis or how well the technologies were researched. An investigation into what would provide the greatest utility for most people, or what tradeoffs most people would be willing make, would show that most would sooner recarpet their home, add a loft room, or move to a better area. Smart home technology will have to be fabulous, failsafe, and relatively cheap (to buy and maintain) before the smart home moves into the mainstream.

> *An innovation almost never serves an entirely new need—the market is always currently being served, however imperfectly, and consumers know how existing alternatives perform and what they cost.*

An innovation almost never serves an entirely new need—the market is always currently being served, however imperfectly, and consumers know how existing alternatives perform and what they cost. Patently, there is a ruthless selection process at work with every innovation, as consumers match them up to what utility they already possess in that area, and what else they have and need, and relentlessly weed out options that do not move them to greater utility. This explains why many products that are theoretically and technically possible never get off the drawing board or out of the labs, that is, don't become part of the future. The old adage, attributed to Ralph Waldo Emerson, that goes: "Build a better mousetrap and the world will beat a path to your door," is right, if by "better" he meant a greater utility mousetrap, considering all angles including price, ease of use, and efficiency. But if better just means technologically more advanced, the wisdom is wrong.

Technology-push forecasting is not just involved with product development. It is also to be found in forecasting services and, more generally, in remedying social and economic ills. Forecasts look forward, for example, to technology's raising crop yields, which will mean fewer people on the planet go hungry, or to advances in environmentally efficient high-speed light rail that will allow people to get out of their cars and take public transport. In reality, we can feed every person on the planet twice over, but that doesn't mean we will. We can make efficient public transport, but that doesn't mean we want to. While the technology-inspired ideal is almost always technically possible, individually or as a society we are often not willing to pay the price or allocate resources to it. The future is never just about what it is possible to do. It is always about the choices people and the market will make from among what we can do.

Of course, to arrive at higher net utility, the additional benefit must outweigh all costs, including transfer costs—the total time, money, and "aggravation" cost of adapting (switching, installing, learning, etc.,) a person or an organization to a new solution. Costs of switching are sometimes called "the installed base" or "legacy systems," that is, what already exists that people have invested time, energy, and money in. The most famous example of an installed base is the qwerty keyboard, originally designed in 1868 to *slow down* typing—separating frequently used pairs of letters on the keyboard in an attempt to stop type bars from intertwining, becoming stuck, and blotting the document. Better keyboards, including the Dvorak keyboard, have been proposed. The cost of replacing keyboards is a factor, but probably not a determining factor. So why are we stuck with an 1868 keyboard? The real and psychological cost of getting hundreds of millions of people to relearn how to touch-type has kept all proposed new keyboards on the drawing board.

Installed base also explains, at least in part, why we still use gasoline in our cars. The persistence of this 100-year-old technology has to do not only with the technical difficulties of powering automobiles by electricity, natural gas, hydrogen, or other technologies, but also with the reality that we are deeply invested in petroleum systems. An alternative energy would require refitting cars, retooling car factories, establishing a new supply chain including pipelines and other support infrastructure, and refitting of gas stations, plus training or retraining of staff all along the supply chain and driver reeducation. It's easy to predict that we will be using alternative or even renewable energy in automobiles, but the reality is that an alternative technology, even if far better, would still have an installed base mountain to climb before total utility becomes positive and it is widely adopted.

Installed base and total utility also explain why, despite forecasts to the contrary, the United States still uses imperial measures and will do so in any foreseeable future. Despite the unassailable fact that metric is more logical and easier to work with (even U.S. scientists and engineers use it), the installed base is high. Americans "think" in imperial measures. All day-to-day systems are calibrated in it. Change would come at enormous cost. And the benefits to the non-scientist are minimal. Therefore, there will be no change.

> *Ignoring the utility principle, including legacy systems, is the key reason for the sad and sorry litany of mistakes in the history of forecasting.*

Ignoring the utility principle, including legacy systems, is the key reason for the sad and sorry litany of mistakes in the history of forecasting. Running a basic market-utility analysis would have wiped out at a stroke most of the silly predictions of the last fifty years and would wipe out most of those being made today. Decoupling prediction from the discipline of consumer utility is like letting go of the neck of an inflated balloon—predictions can fly around the room and bounce off the walls so fast it will make your head spin. Words are cheap, and anything is possible on paper. But no world has ever existed, nor will a world ever exist, where technology determines the future. It is *irrelevant* how hard technology is pushing. If there isn't a corresponding pull from customers, it's a dead letter. It turns out that for anticipating the future as well as everywhere else, the customer is king. (In non-market situations—for example, political dictatorships—there may be ways in which authorities can force a technology into the market. But it is never the technology itself that determines its own adoption.)

The centrality of utility in guiding the future does not mean that technology analysis is an unimportant part of forecasting. It remains highly important, particularly in surfacing the prototypes, possibilities, and options that may create new utility conditions in any field. Technology changes the menu of plausible options that may be put in front of consumers and the businesses that serve them. The impact of evolving technology may not be—and often is not—in new whiz-bang things that might be done at massive cost. It is in the way it affects products, services, and solutions that are on the margins of what is presently done and lowers their price point or other costs (time cost or environment cost or danger, etc.) so that total utility is raised, which brings these marginal solutions within the frame where they will likely be adopted as part of the future.

If we accept that to be part of the future, an innovation must offer utility gain, the questions in understanding the implications of a given technology's progress become if, how, and when the technology will make a genuine rise in consumer utility possible. Not what party tricks a new technology can perform, but what can a new technology offer to tip the cost-benefit balance, to make certain solutions cheaper, or to lower transfer costs to make fringe solutions more attractive than they are currently and therein invite user adoption.

The Fall and Rise of Space Travel

Half a century away— in a different zeitgeist and with the benefit of hindsight—we can see what went wrong in space forecasting and possibly how the space industry will move forward. Forecasters of grand space futures demonstrated a complete failure to think about utility. Once the prestige battle with the Soviets was won and the novelty of knowing someone was on the moon wore off, people across society asked themselves what the benefit of it all was. Poking our noses into cold dark planets in our solar system didn't seem the most important thing to be doing for most people, particularly in the tough "stagflation" 1970s. Nobody was overjoyed about going back for a few more moon rocks or having a couple of guys joyriding across the galaxy on their tax dime. Technology overoptimism and assumptions of "space ambition" or "progress" blinded predictors to the reality that almost everyone would prefer those tax dollars in their own pocket or spent on something that raises their utility, such as better roads or schools.

But space travel of a sort is likely to rise again in our era in the form of commercial "space flips," where people pay to be taken up to experience weightlessness, see the curvature of the earth, and circle the globe. It is far from a certainty, but why will this work where the rest of space travel has foundered? It is, of course, technologically feasible, but, as we have seen, this is merely the first hurdle to future emergence. More important, it gives people something they want. Rightly or wrongly, there is a market desire. And with improved fuel efficiency and other technology advances, the cost-per-head will at some point not be prohibitive. Enough people will feel it is a positive utility experience, not least because of its benefit as a wealth and status marker. Even if it is never be a middle-class thing to do, it will be within reach of many as a special event—a college graduation present, or honeymoon or silver wedding anniversary experience—leading to economies of scale that will bring prices down. Regulation and safety issues would have to be overcome. But all in all, at the balance or forces will likely soon tip and commercial space flips will become part of the future.

Refinements in the Utility Principle

The utility principle is a valuable dependable guide to the future that is particularly able to help us figure out what among the smorgasbord of technology-enabled possibilities will actually emerge and give us some clue how long it will take to reach a point of significance. There are, however, many complexities in the calculation of total utility that forecasts should take into account.

Economies of Scale

As in the example above, the price of a product or service is often subject to economies of scale, which means market adoption in itself lowers price because it is cheaper per unit to produce and supply in bulk. This works in favor of a product over time, but does not exist when the product is introduced. So judging that a utility gain does not exist at present does not mean that a utility gain will not exist in the future, when mass production becomes economically viable. The question then becomes not just "Is this product something that provides value-for-money at present?" It is "Will adoption move the overall cost-benefit point in the future?" or, "Will there be enough initial adoption for the product to evolve to a sustainable cost-benefit point?"

Quality Improves over Time

Similarly, consumer adoption leads to road-testing and feedback, which directly improve product quality. This also does not exist when the product is introduced, but works in favor of the product over time and changes the utility calculation in favor of the innovation and its general adoption. In cases where these price or quality changes occur over time, we typically see a "trickle down" process of future emergence. A product will start at the high end, as a luxury item (providing attractive benefits but at overall low utility gain due to the price—therein more attractive to affluent consumers for whom price sensitivity is lower). As adoption takes place, mass production is able to bring the per-unit price down, raise quality, or both, raising total utility and therefore making the product a substantial part of the future.

> As adoption takes place, mass production is able to bring the per-unit price down, raise quality, or both, raising total utility and therefore making the product a substantial part of the future.

Consumers Have Different Preferences

In judging utility, some will pay more, for example, for the ready convenience of pre-prepared frozen meals; others will pay more for certified organic ingredients. These preferences may be grouped into different market segments, representing different needs and spending profiles. A utility analysis merely asks the overall question: Is utility added to enough segments, such that we can anticipate an innovation will provide a general utility gain, so its widespread emergence may safely be forecast? If it provides utility gain only in a small number of segments, then that too is a guide to the future—it means the product or service implied will emerge to fill a market niche only.

One Group's Highest Utility Outcome Is Not Another's

Different groups—as defined by class, race, nationality, locality, gender, or any other way—may see optimum utility differently. That is, the highest utility solution for one group will not necessarily be the highest for another, and therein political struggles over where and how to allocate resources. A more democratic system will find solutions that provide the highest utility point for most people, most of the time. Where one group has more power, it will be able to create solutions that more closely approximate its own highest total utility point at the expense of others.

Consumers Have Different Price Tolerance or Price "Elasticity"

High price elasticity means the consumer is more sensitive to a price rise and is more likely to switch to another product or avoid purchasing altogether when faced with a price rise. Low elasticity means the customer is less sensitive. In general, consumers are more price elastic on discretionary items than on essentials. Elasticity also correlates with the number of options a consumer has: If she has many options—as with, for example, long distance phone carriers—she will likely be more price elastic and switch to save a few dollars. If, however, she wants an antique fireplace installed and there is only one supplier in the area, a price rise will be absorbed. Elasticity also correlates with whether people are spending their own money. Someone may balk at an overpriced latte, but not if he is on an expense account. Institutional and government spending tends to be less price sensitive than consumer spending, particularly when media and other watchdog organizations are lax.

Price elasticity affects a utility analysis of the future because where elasticity is high a utility analysis becomes even more critical—the odds are heavily stacked against an innovation that doesn't clearly raise user utility. In low-elasticity situations, utility becomes part of the broader set of drivers and blockers that cause the future to emerge or delay its emergence, as discussed in the next chapter.

Social Values May Change over Time

> A utility-led view of the future will be misleading if we assume that what is valuable now will always remain valuable, or that the relative value between items will remain constant.

A utility-led view of the future will be misleading if we assume that what is valuable now will always remain valuable, or that the relative value between items will remain constant. In fact, while some things remain constantly high in value (good health, family, etc.), the generally held value of other things may change over time. For example, the value of metropolitan and highway development has been fairly constant, while value seen in environmental protection has risen sharply. In cases such as this, the cost-benefit implied in a tradeoff (a new metro zone on a piece of land that is an ecological wetland) changes, and society will make different total utility decisions over time. This would explain stiffer regulations to stop development in sensitive ecological spots, and therefore why an regional development forecast that did not account for this would be unreliable.

What Is Cheap or Expensive May Change over Time

We should not be caught up in current standards about what is cheap and what is expensive, what is plentiful and what scarce. If we assume that currently expensive items and processes remain so, and currently cheap or free items remain so, we will miscalculate the changing utility picture. It would have been incorrect in 1960, for example, to assume that the cost of sea and rail freight would stay at the same levels, or that labor (longshoremen) would make up most of that cost. Within a decade, containerization, computerization, and automation plunged the cost of freight to unprecedented levels. Forecasts based on unchanging price patterns would have missed the great rise in international trade and, with it, outsourced production and global supply chains. Similarly, if we were unable to see that international phone calls would plunge in price from 1980 levels—due to privatization and fiber-optic technology, among other things—we would have failed to adequately forecast the spread of everyday national and international telephone-based applications.

An Innovation May Not Successfully Interface with Other Products

> The complementarity between a forecast innovation and the products and procedures consumers are currently invested in is important.

Almost no products or services are used in isolation. For this reason, the complementarity between a forecast innovation and the products and procedures consumers are currently invested in is important. If, for example, a company developed a new material that could be used in plates to keep food hot for the duration of a meal, consumers may like that, but they would also include a "complement index" in deciding whether to buy. They would ask themselves, "Can I put these plates in my existing microwave? Can I wash them in my existing dishwasher?" If not, the new technology likely does not become part of the future. "Futuristic" houses such as geodesic domes sound like a fabulous solution and may be structurally sturdier and environmentally more efficient. But few peoples' furniture fits or looks nice in such a structure. So, despite technological superiority, the total utility gain is not yet positive, and therefore domes are not yet common.

Users will consciously or unconsciously be evaluating whether a change fits with their cultural assumptions and value set—in this case, would a round house be a desirable benefit culturally and emotionally? Will it provide a homely feel? Will it provide status in the neighborhood? If an anticipated innovation does not complement what consumers are already invested in mentally and culturally, in addition to physically and economically, its total utility add will be little or nothing and it will proceed slowly or fail.

Old Products Can Survive with a Different Utility

A utility perspective will lead us to conclude, correctly, that in cases of clear total utility gain a new product or service will emerge and trump the old one. In the example mentioned above, containerization has effectively wiped out loose-pack freight and longshoremen. But seeing a clear utility gain should not lead us to a forecast that the preexisting solution will depart the scene. Often an innovation *adds* to the options available in the world without fully displacing what already exists. The TV didn't replace radio, microwaves didn't replace conventional ovens, cars didn't replaces bicycles or railways or horses, and computers did not replace pen and paper.

> Often an innovation adds to the options available in the world without fully displacing what already exists.

In these and many similar cases the new does not replace the old, it merely adds to the mix, making "all-change" forecasts too simplistic. In forecasting displacement of the old, the forecaster should ask, Does the previous solution have elements of utility that the new solution will not provide, or not at a competitive price? From a utility point of view, the consumer will be asking, What is the real strength of each? And if there are different utilities, both will survive into the future. The bicycle offers exercise that the car does not, as well as different (off-road) recreation opportunities. That is its utility edge, and therefore that will be its core role in future. Bicycles are as popular as they ever were in history, but for a different utility reason.

Once we allow for a "both-and" partial substitution, rather than the "either-or" total substitution, this also lowers the bar for a new solution to enter the world. The new solution does not have to overcome the previous in terms of total utility. The question becomes how readily an aspect of utility or a particular utility *function* that is fulfilled by the previous solution will be replaced by a new solution—and whether or how there would be opposition to that.

Consumers Change the Future . . . Slowly

These various difficulties in making a utility assessment add to its complexity, but should not put us off. Utility is by far our most reliable guide to the future. The future is the future of the many small cost-benefit choices people will make—much more than it is the future of gadgets or grand ideas. Changing an existing utility balance is possible—new technologies do it all the time—but it takes great forces of change, working over a long period of time, to make an innovation widely attractive. Understanding the utility mountain that any innovation must climb in order to overcome and replace the status quo and be an important part of the future gives us a far more dependable and realistic picture of how things will move forward than the wishful thinking and breathless techno-babble to be found in hip magazines. Judging the utility assessment a forecaster has made or

> *Changing an existing utility balance is possible—new technologies do it all the time—but it takes great forces of change, working over a long period of time, to make an innovation widely attractive.*

implied—or failed to make—gives us an unsurpassable jump on assessing the quality of the forecast.

This explains why change moves slowly on average, and why forecasts of change—even where they are right in principle—often massively overestimate the pace and reach of change. The *Batelle Institute*, one of the world's largest enterprises involved in developing and commercialized new technologies, has found that it takes on average twenty years for an innovation to move to commercial status. This has been seen time and time again in the twentieth century. The fax machine was first successfully developed in 1968, but it was only in the mid-1980s that it took off in the market. Microwave ovens were developed twenty years before they reached the market in 1967. The time from a viable gasoline engine to Ford model A, in 1903, was twenty-seven years. Radio technology was viable in 1906, but the first general public radio broadcast was in 1920. The first U.S. television broadcasts were in 1939, seventeen years after television was developed. The computer mouse was developed in 1963, but the first computer to ship with a mouse was the Xerox Star in 1981. The bar code was standardized in 1973, twenty years after the first bar code patent. *Xerox* produced the first copier in 1960, twenty-three years after it filed the patent. The Internet was created by DARPA in the 1970s, and only reached the mass market by the mid to late 1990s.[9]

Dispersion of a predicted innovation across social, cultural, or national boundaries is no certainty either. We should expect separate utility calculations to be made at each place at each point, and different groups or cultures to come to different conclusions, and therefore have different adoption profiles, thus resulting in the future's emerging differently or at different rates across regions. It is a mistake to foresee that a new technology, product, service, preference, or lifestyle will have occurred because it has happened in San Francisco or Berlin, or because it has been adopted by the economic elite, urban youngsters, or any subgroup. Local social, cultural, or economic frictional forces or change blockers may be at work to dampen what appears to be an inevitable change into merely a fad or a niche event. A forecast that claims particularly widespread penetration or diffusion of change must argue first why this will happen at all, and second why it will be widespread. Forecasts for the mobile phone would have passed both those utility tests. But, by default, we should assume the opposite. There is no inevitability about dispersion of a change. A domino effect is commonly assumed, and commonly wrong.

Diffusion of innovation is a field in itself. Its basic theory was formalized by Everett Rogers in *Diffusion of Innovations* (1962), where Rogers determined that the adoptability, and therefore likely diffusion, of an innovation is determined by the following factors:

- Relative Advantage: The degree to which an innovation is perceived as better than the idea it supersedes.
- Compatibility: The degree to which an innovation is perceived as being consistent with existing values, past experiences, and needs of potential adopters.
- Complexity: The degree to which an innovation is perceived as difficult to understand and use.
- Trialability: The degree to which an innovation may be experimented with on a limited basis.
- Observability: The degree to which the results of an innovation are visible to others.

According to Rogers, innovations that are perceived as having greater relative advantage, compatibility, trialability, and observability, while not being overcomplex, will be adopted more rapidly than other innovations. The problem in adopting an innovation is the uncertainty over whether greater benefit—utility in our terms—

will be realized in the adoption. For the risk-averse, utility uncertainty will result in a postponement of the adoption decision until further evidence can be gathered, while the more risk-tolerant will go ahead. Rogers found that a change would first be adopted by innovators (2.5% of the population, on average), followed by "early adopters" (13.5%), then the "early majority" (34%), "late majority" (34%), and "laggards" (16%). Each group's utility uncertainty in adopting change is assuaged by reassuring experiences of the more risk-tolerant group that precedes them, and certain opinion leaders—particularly found in the early adopters group—are able to greatly influence the majority to follow. Nevertheless, even where utility gain turns out to exist and adaptation to the future proceeds as expected, it is still slowed by social and psychological forces of risk intolerance, a further reason why change progresses more slowly than commonly expected.[10]

But not all situations are consumer-driven, and not all futures are as strongly filtered by consumer preference. We consider the wider picture of change drivers and blockers in the next chapter.

Notes

1. The statement was: "I believe that this nation should commit itself to achieving the goal, before this decade is out, of landing a man on the moon and returning him safely to the Earth. No single space project in this period will be more impressive to mankind, or more important for the long-range exploration of space, and none will be so difficult or expensive to accomplish." Speech delivered to joint session of Congress, May 25, 1961. Retrieved May 2008 from www.jfklibrary.org
2. Chicago Public Library. Retrieved November 2006 from www.chipublib.org/004chicago/timeline/skyscraper1.html

3. Retrieved November 2007 from www.infoplease.com/spot/skyscraperhistory.html
4. The total utility calculation can of course include "image and prestige" benefits. Record-breaking buildings today are associated with a national prestige benefit, which makes marginal projects utility-positive to decision makers in countries where that national prestige is sought via building height.
5. Fighter planes are built for a different purpose, but the same principle applies. Beyond a certain speed—about twice the speed of sound—it makes no sense for them to go faster because of human pilot limitations, among other limitations. If technology allowed non-human pilots, then speed can be expected to increase, subject to other limitations, for example, fuel cost or material tolerances.
6. Speculative thinking and laboratory initiatives to increase airline speed are under way all the time. For one example, see "The hypersonic plane designed to reach Australia in under 5 hours," *The Guardian* (February 15, 2008). www.guardian.co.uk/business/2008/feb/05/theairlineindustry.travelnews
7. B. Seidensticker, *Future Hype* (San Francisco: BK, 2006).
8. S. Schnaars, *Megamistakes* (New York: Free Press, 1989), p. 53. Schnaars provides an excellent, detailed study of the numerous technology-driven forecasts that are failed prophecies.
9. Quoted in Seidensticker., op. cit.
10. E. Rogers, *Diffusion of Innovations* (New York: Free Press, 1962).

CHAPTER 6

Drivers, Blockers, and Trends

IN THE PREVIOUS CHAPTER WE IDENTIFIED USER utility as a key condition in the success or failure of change. We now integrate this into a broader model of change drivers and blockers and consider problems in trend extrapolation.

What Is a Trend?

A trend is a sequential pattern of change in recorded data—a change evidenced by a rise or fall of variables when measured between at least two points over time. If we can see (measure) that housing starts have fallen every year for the past five years, we have a trend. If we see more couples marrying later in life in 2008, compared with 1958, we have a trend. To be commonly considered a trend, rather than a fad or a blip, a pattern in the data must pass basic tests of significance; it must be a change that affects a wide range of people and that has, or will eventually have, broad social, economic, or political implications. Fads are transient or narrow in scope and affect only particular social groups or regions, without long-term implications. Fads typically spread quickly but disappear equally quickly. The empowerment of women in Western societies over the course of the twentieth century was a trend. The rise and fall of CB radios in the 1970s was a fad. Elmo dolls were a fad, but "lite" beer is part of an overall trend (to healthier, fitter lifestyles).

> To be commonly considered a trend, rather than a fad or a blip, a pattern in the data must pass basic tests of significance; it must be a change that affects a wide range of people and that has, or will eventually have, broad social, economic, or political implications.

Trends overlap and interlock, reinforcing each other. For example, urbanization is a major trend all over the world, related to and boosted by other trends, particularly the influence of Western lifestyles, and nations integrating into the global economy and global supply chains, where jobs are for the most part in cities. Trends can also run counter to each other and cancel each other out. In the U.S. wine industry, for example, the trend is toward wine drinking (for health benefits among other reasons), but away from alcohol as a whole, has left wine consumption levels more or less flat.

Sometimes trends are strong enough to cause their own backlash or "counter-trend"—that is, they stimulate forces in opposition to the original trend. For example, the worldwide rise of an educated, secular, consumerist middle class is one of the strongest trends of our era. The planet has become more integrated by Western middle-class values than at any point in human history. However, at the same time, and undeniably at least partly due to this trend, we also see the rise of anti-globalization forces, and, separately, the renewing of reactionary religious fundamentalism.

Horizon Scanning

Trend recognition or "trend tracking" begins with environmental or horizon scanning, the process of seeking out and gathering information at the margins of current perception. Scanning looks and listens for new ideas and new practices that are the straws in the wind of change. The term borrows from military or naval scanning of the horizon—looking for distant objects or "weak signals" that give early warning of changes in the environment.

Therefore, the first demand of scanning is breadth. It sweeps as wide a spectrum of sources as possible in order to reveal events on the periphery of what is commonly known and commonly thought important.

Scanners will particularly look to fringe media where new ideas are more likely to make their first emergence. For example, while AIDS was not discernable as an issue on network television and in national newspapers until well into the 1980s, it was being reported far earlier in medical journals and in special-interest urban magazines. In the same vein, scanners with their ear to the ground would have seen energy deregulation or just-in-time production, or any of hundreds of world-shaking changes, before they hit the mainstream. Early identification is key to the process: There is competitive advantage in noticing new forces earlier than others or being able to assemble a fuller picture of what is coming before others do. Trend spotters pride themselves on being able to "call" a trend before anyone else.

The best scanners aren't content with secondary sources and go on "learning journeys" directly to people or places where portentous events may be happening. Quality scanning is also not just cognizant of what people say or write, but also what they do. Scanning may therefore consider the spin of a government spokesman lightly, while weighing the number of protest callers, dollars donated, or staff resignations heavily. As ever, actions speak louder than words.

In theory, scanning precedes trend tracking, but in practice, as soon as weak-signal material is gathered, it is analyzed and contextualized for trend significance. From each new event or data point the analyst will be asking, Does this fit a pattern? Is this suggestive of a trend? Is this part of a bigger phenomenon, a growth or decline of significance that will change the operating environment, offering threats and opportunities and changing what is required of organizations in order to be successful?

Problems in Trend Recognition

As we saw in Chapter 4, forecasters bring their cognitive filters and conscious and unconscious biases to bear in perceiving the world. Trend recognition is, similarly, a cognitive construct. A trend is not there until someone defines it. What "appears" or is recognized on any one person's or organization's horizon scan, and how it is categorized and interpreted is obviously deeply subject to cognitive and paradigm filters. Some patterns—for example, an aging population—are relatively easy to see and nobody would contest their interpretation. But if the evidence is unclear, the way of counting or measuring the data is contended, or the results could be viewed or defined in different ways, a trend's existence will be less clear. Is there, for example, currently a trend to reading books electronically? It depends on definitions and on what is measured. Different analysts will often observe the data differently or group it differently or make different choices in trend "smoothing," to the point where some see a trend while others will see no trend or a different trend. In this way, identification of a trend is often a judgment call and subject to the biases discussed in the previous chapter.

> *The propensity to see a trend may be the result of partisan situations, where the interests of different groups may make them more willing to identify it.*

The propensity to see a trend may be the result of partisan situations, where the interests of different groups may make them more willing to identify it. For example, the trend to global warming, for all that it appears valid and clear, is beset with debates about what to count, how to count it, and how to interpret the findings—all of which become factors in how valid and how steep the trend is seen to be, which influences the policy. In many cases such as this, the issue is less the ability to see a trend than the willingness to see it.

Projecting Trends

With these caveats, as trends are revealed, the logical next step is to ask, "Where is this trend heading in the future?" Trend-based projection is the bread and butter of forecasting and by far the most common basis of prediction among professional and lay forecasters. Its intuitive logic is very powerful and, moreover, rests on empirical justification: We can see something growing or dissolving (at least in the data) before our eyes, and we can verify the rate at which it is happening. If there were 165,000 people living in Las

Vegas in 1980, 260,000 in 1990, and 480,000 in 2000, we intuit a growth trend, and we feel halfway to a valid forecast. Extrapolation of past data is also reassuringly amenable to quantitative calculations. Once we can compute the rate of growth for Las Vegas, it is then a simple step to achieving a prediction by extrapolating that growth rate to 2020 or 2040.

Trend projection is also "agnostic." It does not ask *why* a trend is moving. It only notices that it is moving and extends this movement into the future. It allows us to bypass the causes of events and behavior that may be tricky to identify or agree on. We don't have to debate open-ended questions such as *why* people are choosing to settle in Vegas, who they are, or what they are doing there. We can just record that the trend exists and follow this to the future.

If forecasting were as simple as extrapolating in this mechanical way, it would be an easy game indeed. The problem with trend projection is it assumes a decline will keep on declining or a rise rising, and at the same rate. It assumes the future will be a logical extension of the past. It runs into trouble when the assumptions of continued trend line behavior are incorrect, that is, when new factors cause the trend to change or reverse. If even one key assumption shifts slightly, the forecast goes badly wrong. In fact, one incorrect assumption easily trumps all the careful data collection and meticulous projection, and the forecast will be out by miles, not inches. When underlying conditions change, trend extrapolations instantly become ridiculous.

In forecasting circles the story is told about concerned policymakers in Victorian London toward the end of the nineteenth century, looking at population growth trends for the city, who were concerned about rising levels of horse manure in the streets. At the time manure could be inches deep in places, but, if current trends continued, by 1910 it would be ankle deep, and by 1925 London would be knee deep in dung. This didn't happen. What happened was the development of the internal combustion engine and the automobile, which changed the assumption that horses were involved in transportation. Once the car appeared, all forecasts based on horse-drawn transportation were not slightly wrong, they were ridiculous.

Drivers, Enablers, Friction, and Blockers

Trend extrapolation gets itself into this kind of a mess precisely because a trend is an identified pattern in the data, and no more. It is the *evidence* of forces of change and makes these forces visible to research and analysis, but it is not those forces and sometimes tells us little about them. The forces of change behind a trend, commonly called *change drivers*, are what underpin trends and make them what they are. The trend to, for example, hybrid mixed-fuel automobiles is "driven" by change drivers such as higher gas prices and environmental concerns. (A driver can of course underpin many different trends.) The aging trend is driven by advances in medicine, better access to healthcare on average, healthier lifestyles, improved general education levels, and so on. In these cases, and in every case, trends are merely the visible evidence of change drivers at work.[1]

> The forces of change behind a trend, commonly called change drivers, *are what underpin trends and make them what they are.*

While a change driver is a force for change, an *enabler* is a factor that promotes or facilitates a driver, for example, government laboratory funding, venture capital backing, intellectual property protection, or the free market system as a whole, which may facilitate the emergence of a new technology. *Friction* is the resistance to change that occurs naturally and

> Friction *is the resistance to change that occurs naturally and inevitably due to, for example, legacy systems or embedded procedures or learned habits or existing legislation.*

inevitably due to, for example, legacy systems or embedded procedures or learned habits or existing legislation. As we saw in the previous chapter, consumers will always judge innovations against the current way they do things, and people are socially and culturally invested in known, familiar patterns that take a lot to overcome. It is often more convenient and less risky to do things the old way. This status quo inertia is an inherent stickiness or "friction" against change.

> Blockers *are the forces that actively oppose a change.*

Finally, *blockers* are the forces that actively oppose a change. Blockers may take the form of new legislation, political filibustering, preventive buyouts, protesters in the street, or other factors. They occur when people try to stop a change or delay it (sometimes to buy time to shape what emerges). Blockers are often found in political or industry forces. For example, it was medically clear that smoking was a health hazard and a major government health expense from the mid-1960s. The future was clearly against tobacco. Yet the tobacco industry was able to block the inevitable for more than thirty years. A forecast that did not factor in power to block and shape outcomes would have grossly overestimated how long it took before smoking became socially and legally unacceptable. Similarly, a forecast of normalization of U.S.-Cuba relations would be worthless if it did not explain how the blocking force of U.S. Cuban émigrés would be overcome.

Blockers may also be seen in human or materials tolerances, safety concerns, or other social mores. For example, the GM exhibit at the 1939 World's Fair foresaw a continued rise in *average* automobile speed to "100 mph by 1960," projecting forward the then-current speed gain trend. It did not account for limitations of human sensory systems, safety and insurance considerations, tolerances of materials, fuel consumption ethics (or cost), and traffic congestion, all of which have been blockers of automobile speed.

We can thus conceive of the future as forces for change—change drivers and enablers—working in opposition to forces acting against it—friction and blockers. What will come about is the net effect of these forces, the evolving accommodation that results from change drivers and enablers meeting resistance and blockers. Real lasting change occurs if and when drivers overpower blockers. In situations where much is at stake, and powerful forces stand to lose if a trend runs, those forces will counter the trend. If labor unions were to grab more power, chances are business forces would counter them politically or through legislation. If a new food additive is shown to be a significant factor in child obesity, it will, one way or another be removed. Forecasts that merely march the trend forward without anticipating countering forces will be wrong.

Of all the factors, blockers are often the hardest to see or may only emerge in the fullness of time. Oftentimes, however, analysts—particularly those keen to see the future before anyone else—extrapolate marginal or early-stage trends without adequately considering frictional or blocking forces. A good forecast will consider blockers and not assume that because nothing appears to be in the way of an innovation now, nothing will block it downstream. A worthwhile forecast will consider the resources and time required to overcome blockers, and motivate how they will be overcome, as a routine part of forecasting a change.

In the previous chapter we identified a rise in user utility as driver of change (in favor of the higher-utility solution) and a fall in utility as a blocker. Alongside utility, the following are the major categories of driving forces and blockers:

- **Technology.** Technology is without doubt the most powerful force for change in the world. It provides new capabilities that change what is possible in products and services, as well as in operational solutions and business models. Better technologies alter the utility equation, allowing us to do more for less, and therein make changes to how we do things. But technology evolution is also sometimes, in itself, a blocker of change, particularly where a solution cannot be created. For example, the technological difficulties in creating "artificial intelligence" have been immense—far greater than anticipated—and this has put the brakes on the future in this area.

- **Powerful individuals and powerful organizations.** Throughout history, powerful or charismatic figures from Jesus to Hitler have changed the future. Typically, kings and presidents, celebrities, and well-connected individuals have the influence and following to achieve this. Often, the force of individuals is combined with the institutional power of government, military, or corporate power. Some institutions in banking, the media, or pharmaceuticals may become powerful enough to drive trends or block them. Without overplaying conspiracy theory, it is obvious that powerful forces or "vested interests," whether corporate, political, or military, are often heavily invested in the status quo and may use their resources directly, or behind the scenes, acting to prevent outcomes that would be detrimental to their interests.

- **Ideas and ideologies.** We act in accordance with our ideas and ideologies, and these therefore drive social, political, economic, and technological choices for the future. Driving or blocking ideas and ideologies may be classic ideas such as democracy or "the rule of law," or new ideas such as environmentalism or political correctness. Ideas may be visionary and aspirational, seeking to change the future toward an ideal, or fear-based, changing current trends in order to avoid things we stand for being crushed. Often different ideas and ideologies are in conflict with each other, causing a political clash over what kind of future would be more ideal. Ideas and ideologies are also vulnerable to social currents or propaganda and shift with the zeitgeist over time. This means that trend-driving ideas may strengthen or weaken, changing the force underpinning or countering a trend.

- **Social and moral values.** These are related to ideas, of course, but have a slightly different function because values generally change very slowly, if at all, so they mostly apply brakes on the future. Often social values are the "last line of defense" against a rush of technology capabilities that may or may not lead us to questionable places. There are many things we can do—cloning humans, for example—where we are asking ourselves, is this what we *want* to do? As with ideologies, different social groups and different societies, representing different values, may make different choices, so values conflicts surface over whether we should block the future. Often social values are institutionalized in the form of regulation, where the courts or government (in response to public opinion) will enforce a position that may block the future.

Obviously, this is a very high-level list. Each category breaks down into many subcategories and factors that will have change-driving or blocking properties. A good forecast will investigate each of these categories, and provide a sense of the balance of power for and against the trend.

The Benefits of a Driver-Level Analysis

Understanding the forces that promote or retard trends allows us a more sophisticated view of where a trend will go in the future. Particularly, it allows us to see the following attributes of change.

Trend Breaks and Inflection Points

> Understanding a trend as a reflection of underlying driving and blocking forces explains why trends are capable of the sudden surprises and reversals we see around us.

Understanding a trend as a reflection of underlying driving and blocking forces explains why trends are capable of the sudden surprises and reversals we see around us. A trend has no life of its own. It is only as dependable as its drivers. If a new force emerges, the trend will stop or change. It is a candy wrapper in the wind. When the wind stops, the wrapper stops. This should make us extremely hesitant to forecast by extrapolating a trend. To do so is to assume the continued strength of current underlying drivers and continued status quo in the driver-blocker "force field." In fact, given the action of many drivers and blockers determining any trend, it is always more likely there will be a new, yet unseen factor that stops the extrapolated future from happening as expected, or that accelerates or reverses it. A forecast that proceeds by extrapolating trends is only worth taking seriously if it identifies the underlying drivers of change and makes a cogent case that these drivers are durable into the future.

In 1910, in the early history telephony, a Bell telephone statistician projected a massive ramp-up in switchboard operator jobs as telephone use grew, until "every woman in America" would be required. This forecast projected the rapidly growing telephone service, therefore a growing demand for live operators, but missed automated switching, which fundamentally changed the need for live operators. Automated switching was the new factor, the trend breaker. It fundamentally changed the validity of the assumption on which the extrapolation rested, no doubt to the surprise of the forecaster and everyone who based his or her thinking or financial or technology investments on this forecast.

Such breaks or inflection points (also known as "discontinuities")[2] are hard for trend-based forecasting to account for precisely because anticipating trend inflection points can only be done by investigating the unseen force field driving and/or blocking a trend. Inflection-probing questions would be: How may a driver gather new strength, or new drivers or enablers be co-opted, to be able to overcome existing blockers? Or how may new blockers emerge to stymie an expected change? What are the key turning points that will change the balance between drivers and blockers and how might an outside event change the balance of power?

The Changing Pace of Change

In addition to missing trend breaks, if a trend-based forecast does not investigate the underlying force field, it will be prone to also mistakenly implying a constant pace of change. Trend extrapolation almost inevitably gives the illusion of a dependable rate of change, a steady growth or wane through stages that unfold in a smooth and rational manner toward a future state. But even where trends do evolve as expected—where trend breaks and reversals do not occur—they often seldom evolve at the expected rate. There are accelerations or slow-downs as the balance between drivers and blockers shifts. In other words, the underlying force field not only determines whether a change comes about, but the pace of change and how this pace may vary. The visible trend line tells us nothing about when the acceleration or deceleration will come, or how great it will be, or how long it will last.

In a static situation, by definition, the total force of drivers and enablers is equal to the countering force of friction and blockers. Where we have a steady transition—a trend—change drivers and enablers are slowly overcoming friction and blockers. Where drivers and enablers are strong and blockers are weak, we can expect the pace of change to be rapid and even, under extreme conditions, exponential. Where blockers are strong, we should expect them to nullify change altogether.

Sometimes change is held back or proceeds slowly due to one blocker, which is, as scientists term it, the "rate-limiting factor." If this factor is removed, the future will move forward, or move at a greater pace. When change "suddenly" occurs, or is noticeable, it is often the case that an outside event has shaken the relationship between forces for and against a change. A new source of funding, a legislative development, an assassination, or a new scientific discovery is the kind of development that can unblock the future or reverse a running trend. The likelihood of a trend-break event increases as the forecast period increases, making trend extrapolation less reliable the further into the future it is extrapolated.

The Power of the Status Quo

It is common in the early twenty-first century to see change as a "constant" in society and to expect and plan for the rush of the new. One of the insights of the force field model is to recognize that seeing change as a natural, default, or inevitable state is spurious. In fact, while change comes and goes in (sometimes strong) waves, it is not inevitable. Ironically, *resistance* to change is inevitable. As Newton's first law, the Law of Inertia, states: "An object at rest will remain at rest unless acted upon by an external force. An object in motion will remain in motion unless acted upon by an external force." It may seem a stretch to apply a scientific law to the muddy waters of human social and economic affairs, but it makes perfect intuitive and practical sense and is borne out by experience. Nothing in the world changes unless a force or a collection of forces acts on it, and nothing moves

> While change comes and goes in (sometimes strong) waves, it is not inevitable. Ironically, resistance to change is inevitable.

unless the forces of change overwhelm inertia (and blocking forces). We don't need reasons to expect continuation of the status quo, we only need reasons to show how and where it will be overcome.

It is not enough that a forecast gives us a well-researched, well-reasoned picture of how things will change, it must also in the first instance give us compelling reasons *why* things will change at all. In the absence of any force of change that will overwhelm both friction and blockers, we should expect the status quo to continue. Unless persuaded otherwise, our default assumption should be "no change."

Systemic Interactions and Complexity

> Perhaps the biggest problem of all in trend projection is that it implies we can separate out the single variable we are interested in and roll it forward, without allowing for the complexity of how all the other variables affect the picture.

Perhaps the biggest problem of all in trend projection is that it implies we can separate out the single variable we are interested in and roll it forward, without allowing for the complexity of how all the other variables affect the picture. Economists and scientists use the Latin term *ceteris paribus* (the rest remains the same) when thinking through the effect of one change. Business uses the term "sensitivity analysis" when trying to isolate the effect of changing one variable. But in the real world, of course, everything else does not remain the same. The rest of the world does not stand still, so no trend can be expected to run without influence from others. The real world is systemically more complex than any single trend extrapolation can account for.

A famous example of extrapolating a single trend while failing to account for broader systemic forces were the various 1970s' forecasts that asserted the world was "running out of oil." The then-current rising oil consumption trend was put against known reserves, leaving a simple calculation as to what year oil would run dry. These oil forecasts did not take into account forces in favor of improved discovery and recovery of oil, or more efficient refining. As *Scientific American* reflected in 1998, "Those energy experts did not foresee the advances in supercomputers and geophysics that allow satellite-based exploration; advances in materials science and engineering that permit unprecedented construction of multibillion-dollar oil platforms in waters more than a mile deep; (and) advances in robotics that permit operations in hostile and deep waters."[3] In fact, decades later it is now estimated that there is more oil in the ground than was thought in the 1970s, despite the world today using it at the rate of 22 million barrels per day.[4]

In focusing on one trend, the forecaster cannot assume that other elements that affect it will be constant and not (a) respond to the trend and (b) respond to each other, setting in motion further changes all of which will cumulatively affect the total net outcome. A systems dynamics perspective—the topic of Chapter 8—helps us expect and account for situations where drivers of change do not lead to expected outcomes because the system acts to change, reinforce, or counterbalancing them. Before this, we take a look at quantitative modeling, an elaboration of trend extrapolation that uses statistical tools and computers to forecast the future behavior of many interacting trends.

Notes

1. It is often confusing that these underlying drivers and enablers are themselves trends, or commonly expressed as trends. If we see more couples delaying marriage and children, that is trend evidence of underlying forces—more women working, or the changing needs in the economy, particularly the need for more

higher skilled work requiring longer qualification periods. The quest for higher qualifications is a trend, which is based on the kinds of jobs available in Western economies—that in itself is a trend based on underlying geopolitical and geoeconomic forces. In this way, we often have "trend layering," where a driving force creates a trend and that trend is the driving force of another trend.

2. Some analysts of change refer to a "punctuated equilibrium" model, wherein a sudden event or mutation creates an abrupt new path, setting in motion a new trend. The trend then defines the period following dislocation from one equilibrium and preceding a return to a new equilibrium.
3. "The End of Cheap Oil: Back to the Future." *Scientific American* (March, 1998).
4. Retrieved March 2008 from www.gravmag.com/oil.html

CHAPTER 7

The Limits of Quantitative Forecasting

IN THE PREVIOUS CHAPTER WE DISCUSSED PROBLEMS with trend extrapolation as an approach to future prediction. But we dealt essentially with problems in single-issue projection. Is it not perhaps possible to consider the simultaneous interaction of many variables, perhaps with a complex statistical model backed by computer power, and so achieve a trend projection we can rely on? In this chapter we consider where this is possible and useful, and where it is not.

Statistical Analysis and Quantitative Modeling

Our lives and decisions are dominated by statistics. For better or worse, quantitative analysis has become *the* authoritative form of knowledge. In fact, this is a relatively new phenomenon in the history of human thought. It is only since the nineteenth century that statistical analysis has come to stand at the core of the way we think about the world, and alternative forms of investigation—judgment, experience, and intuition—have been pushed into the background. But the pendulum has swung so far that, in our era, not only have quantitative approaches become central to how we investigate complex situations, but also unless something is numerically studied, it is almost "not knowledge." Economics, once an arena of social analysis, has become a field of turbo-math, while management academics produce papers that more closely resemble particle physics than anything real managers actually do. This pattern is repeated across much of psychology and the rest of the social sciences.

Ready access to computer power, allowing us to do more with numbers, has greatly facilitated this shift. So it should come as no surprise that many people look to statistical analysis or quantitative methods, and particularly computer-driven projective modeling, to solve the conundrum of predicting the future. Software developers and entrepreneurs have taken up the challenge to develop computer-driven forecasting methodologies with alacrity. Future-oriented number-crunching software programs, with such names as *Autocast, ForecastX, Forecast Pro,* and *SmartForecasts,* are often lavishly advertised to corporations and other institutions that have

> *So it should come as no surprise that many people look to statistical analysis or quantitative methods, and particularly computer-driven projective modeling, to solve the conundrum of predicting the future.*

an interest in anticipating and evaluating change. *Forecast Pro*'s advertising text is typical of the kind: "With Forecast Pro, you provide the historic data for the items you are forecasting and Forecast Pro does the rest. The built-in expert selection mode analyzes your data, selects the appropriate forecasting technique and calculates the forecasts using proven statistical methods."[1]

All computer-driven quantitative modeling generates future projections through predictive algorithms, based on mathematical relationships between variables derived from analysis of past data. Patterns and associations among variables and multiple relationships of cause and effect (causal and dependent variables) may be derived, for example, by regression techniques, to determine what mix of causal influences are at work on any perceived outcome variable, and the degree of influence of each on the outcome. (A slump in sales may be attributed to many factors: less advertising, placement of outlets, lower consumer spending, competitive influences, distributor discounts, product options, changes in household income, etc. A regression can help determine what mix of causal factors in what proportion has caused this over time.)

Modeling techniques, including econometrics, set the deduced coefficients between variables into complex algorithms that mathematically define the relationships between variables and set decision points about which variables affect which others, under what conditions, and by how much. With this, the modeler can project into future time, allowing us to watch the future evolving on a computer screen.

The most common form of quantitative projection is based on a "time-series analysis," where a sequence of data points measured at successive and preferably uniform time intervals has been collected. Using the standard measure of time as a base, analysts create a mathematical curve that approximates the data evolution to the present, sometimes using moving averages or other data-smoothing techniques. If, for example, new car purchases in southern Germany are connected to an expansion of the Munich job market year by year, a time-series analysis is able to plot a trajectory for this. As long as time is considered to be a determining force, and the relationship between time and the dependent variable is assumed to hold, the analysis can project the value of the dependent variable forward in time. The forecaster can say that given continuing conditions, car sales will follow this known trajectory. When asked to forecast the future of car sales in the region, the forecaster will be able to run the model forward to find the answer. Sometimes modeling factors are slightly varied to give a "high," "medium," and "low" result, or a "best-case" and "worst-case" projection.

The math behind this is complex and impressive, and models are often presented with animated graphs showing interactions and transformations in speeded-up time, creating an undeniable "wow effect." It is beyond the scope or intention of this book to assess the approaches of this software in mathematical or programming terms. There is no question that as a whole these approaches are mostly enacted correctly in their own terms. And, as explained further below, forecasts that are data rich and quantitatively derived do better than intuitive or judgmental methods in many situations. The intention here is rather to understand where quantitative predictions work, and where and why they stop being useful, to find the limits to this approach, which will guide us in judging the merits of a forecast. Our question about predictive modeling will not be "is it valid?" but, "has it been applied in the correct situation?" To see what the computer algorithms are really up against, we have to investigate the problem of complexity a little further.

> Our question about predictive modeling will not be "is it valid?" but, "has it been applied in the correct situation?"

The Limits of Determinism: Chaos, Complexity, and Wicked Problems

In the eighteenth century, social theorists thought the laws of human behavior were deterministic, like laws of physics, and that a "science of society" was possible. It has since become clear that no deterministic laws govern human actions or society. It is one thing to be able to determine the fertility of fruit flies because the number of factors that affect their fertility may reasonably be known and accounted for within a closed system. It is another thing altogether to have data completeness with regard to human and social situations that are multifactorial, where we don't understand all the variables or the complex interaction between them. For a "science" of human society to be possible, such knowledge would be necessary, including a detailed knowledge of a starting point (initial conditions), plus a clear and exhaustive exposition of the forces driving the status quo and a complete knowledge of how they interact.

It turns out these are effectively impossible conditions even in considering the present, let alone the future. We cannot claim in every instance that a force will lead clearly to an expected change or not to an unexpected change. This invalidates any effort to deterministically predict human events. Marketing analyst Pat LaPointe gives a graphic example: "Even though baseball statisticians have over 100 years of data loaded into high-speed computers at their fingertips, the human element in what happens with the very next pitch makes it nearly impossible to forecast (with any acceptable accuracy) who will win *the game*, never mind the pennant."[2]

Therefore, there can be no science of human society or human institutions, nor "scientific" prediction of its future. In the science-of-society debate, philosopher Karl Popper definitively pronounced, "There can be no prediction of the course of human history by scientific or any other rational methods. . . . We must reject the possibility of social science that would correspond to theoretical physics."[3] Acknowledging this fundamental complexity at the heart of human and natural affairs has spurred non-deterministic models of how the world works. Chaos theory (often coupled with complexity theory) originated in the natural sciences, but has quickly been absorbed into economics and social sciences to help account for rule-based, yet ultimately unfathomable changes.

Chaos theory analysts have also postulated immense sensitivity to changes in initial conditions, the so-called "butterfly effect," where small changes or chance events can lead to widely differing outcomes when fully played out, due to the unfathomable complexity of multiple and often reinforcing forces. Apparently inconsequential events, even someone forgetting her keys and turning round to get them, can lead them to be in the wrong place at the wrong time and entirely change her future. A chance word or a stray bullet can change history. Billions of small changes are happening all around us all the time, and the immensity of their effects when played out make it impossible to foresee outcomes with any confidence. Also, while chaotic situations do exhibit underlying patterns or perform in regular, predictable ways under certain conditions, under other conditions regularity and predictability is lost.

> Billions of small changes are happening all around us all the time, and the immensity of their effects when played out make it impossible to foresee outcomes with any confidence.

Other ways of expressing irreducible complexity have also gained currency, for example, the concept of a "wicked problem," proposed by Rittel and Webber to describe situations that have incomplete, ill-defined, or systemically contradictory interdependent variables (contrasted to "tame" problems where there is one clear solution even if it may be hard to find.)[4] *There is no solution* to a wicked problem. Such a problem is solved, if it is solved at all, by acting on multiple fronts at once. Along similar lines, Malcolm Gladwell, citing U.S. national-security expert Greg Treverton, distinguishes between "puzzles" and "mysteries." A puzzle is a problem that lacks information, and if that information were provided, it could be solved. In mysteries, however, more information or more information processing doesn't necessarily help. As Gladwell says, "Sometimes the information we've been given is inadequate, and sometimes we aren't very smart about making sense of what we've been given, and sometimes the question itself cannot be answered."[5] Apparently, even the U.S. military has bought into a nondeterministic type of explanatory framework, using the acronym VUCA (Volatile, Uncertain, Complex, and Ambiguous) to describe the world we live in.[6]

For our purposes, all of these analytic terms for hypercomplex situations amount to the same thing. They describe problems that are beyond the deterministic framework, that have no simple analytical fix, *no matter how hard we try*. Predicting the future is this kind of problem. For these reasons, no matter how sophisticated-seeming the quantitative approach, or how expensive the software, or how pretty the color images, underneath the swirl of projected numbers and their elegant presentation, unsolvable problems remain.

These are the particular questions of a computer-driven forecast that claims to predict the future.

- **Is the data good?** The various problems with data are described extensively in Chapter 2, and following the analysis we know that the "hard" numbers fed into any statistical model are and always will be subject to the "art" of human judgment. Some data sets will be better than others, but none is perfect. A quantitative forecast depends first on the quality of the numbers—both historical and present—as its forecast base and if it's "garbage-in" it can only be "garbage-out." Also, the person or team who builds the quantitative forecast model may manipulate the input numbers further or screen out outliers or those considered less likely. In the terms described in Chapter 3, this may be willful bias, but it may equally be unconscious choices, that is, a point of view at work.

- **Have we taken all factors into consideration?** If human systems are overpoweringly complex, the next question is whether the model has accounted for all the factors that influence the future—the factor inputs. As the number of variables and length of time increases, the problem is that we can *never* fully account for all the factors that are causing or resisting change in the situation we are trying to predict. For example, in considering the future of the cruise vacation industry, one may consider factors in the economy, lifestyle, demographics, competing industries—but which factors are included and which are not? Also, what about other factors, for example, terrorism, oil prices, the spread of English, and so on? There is never a point where we can be sure we have accounted for all the drivers of change in any situation under study. We may, from time to time, be able to see a clear driver of change doing apparently predictable things, but that driver may be acting on existing conditions we don't fully see, or be blocked by elements we don't fully recognize, or otherwise part of a not fully conceivable system. A quantitative model is a necessarily simplified representation of a reality. There are always more inputs than can be grasped, let alone programmed.

> A quantitative model is a necessarily simplified representation of a reality. There are always more inputs than can be grasped, let alone programmed.

⋄ **What affects what, when, at what rate, and by how much?** If we are satisfied that the model analysis is based on good data, and that it has completeness of factor inputs, we still run up against the problem of how to quantify cause and effect. In other words, what influences what in the model, under what conditions, at what rate, and by how much? To make a good quantitative prediction, the forecaster must determine what these relationships are in order to be able to enter them as coefficients and algorithms that tell the model how to calculate the way each changing variable affects others over time. Every mathematical relationship between two data points represents an assumption. For example, if we decide that the doubling of factory development will lead to a 40% increase in road use, we have made an assumption. We may have grounds for this, such as expert opinion or past evidence, but it remains an assumption that may or may not represent the future relationship between two variables. Algorithms apply multiple assumptions about the evolution, interaction, and mutation of variables, and for an algorithm to be valuable, every assumption must be correct.

In a short but appropriately severe essay, titled "Why We Can't Predict," author Neil Duncan divides the problems that must be solved to get to good algorithms and therefore good forecasts, into four types—shape, thresholds, interactions, and lag. *Shape* refers to the mathematical form of the relationship between input factors and output (the future predicted), which may vary from a simple straight line to a relationship that "needs half a page of algebra to describe it." *Thresholds* are discontinuities in relationships, where the effect of an input factor suddenly changes. All values below a threshold may be zero, but above the threshold the factor influences events enormously and may cause a system to change entirely or collapse. Obviously, we can rarely tell where the threshold is going to be.

Interactions are present when the effect of a factor depends on the values of one or more of the other factors. As "everything affects everything," our ability to forecast is commensurately reduced as the number of interconnections and interactions rises—to an effectively unfathomable total complexity. *Lag* takes place when output is affected not by the current value of a factor but by an earlier or later value, which raises the problem of how far back to go in considering pertinent inputs. (Lag itself may be subject to interactive or threshold effects.) In any human social system, each of these four factors is effectively uncontainable, making outcome possibilities unlimited and therein impossible to forecast.[7]

- **Will the assumption hold through the forecast period?** If the model has good data, completeness of factor inputs, and we're satisfied that it has somehow managed to make the right assumptions and correctly model the unfathomable complexity of the present, there is still the problem of whether its assumptions will continue to be correct. The algorithms at best mimic past relationships between variables, but for the forecast to be right these assumptions as to the fact and extent of causality must hold through the forecast time period. Assumptions, as we have seen in Chapter 5, are based on underlying beliefs, mental models, or a zeitgeist that may or may not reflect future reality. Our current mental model will more likely be good for one year ahead than, say, ten years out, so the further into the future we try to look, the less dependable our present assumptions will be.

  If assumptions about future causality are not good, the forecast cannot be good, no matter how good the rest of the forecast process is. *Cisco,* for example, is a company renowned for its sophisticated data-driven predictive inventory management system that incorporates market, supply chain, and competitor data. Yet it had to take an estimated $2.2 billion inventory write-off and enforce huge layoffs when forecast modelers failed to take into account the dot.com bust and subsequent recession in the industry in 2001. All the modeling in the world did not help Cisco because its assumptions became invalid. Worse, as is commonly the case, the predictive results had the veneer of hard factuality, only to be all the more misleading because of this. Lulled by the extent and quality of their data, and the rigors of the forecast process, the company was unwilling or unable to question fundamental assumptions of the 1990s that ceased to be valid well within their forecast horizon.

Distinguishing Between Levels of Uncertainty

These problems of complexity in forecasting are borne out again and again by the many weak forecasts and forecast errors we are all witness to. The evidence shows we can't reliably quantify the future in any situation of real complexity, and now we understand why. However, common practice also shows that quantitative methods are used very effectively to make predictions about short-term business or policy variables. The methods are used and found useful every day in every industry and throughout government policy and planning. So how are we to understand this apparent paradox?

Hugh Courtney and fellow authors have developed an analysis of levels of uncertainty that helps us out.[8] In setting up their analysis, Courtney et al., McKinsey consultants, report the struggle that the consulting firm—and by extension similar blue-chip strategy consulting firms and the companies and governments they work for—have had in dealing with a fast-changing world. As they report, during the 1990s, they became acutely aware of the failure of standard industry analysis tools to helpfully analyze high-uncertainty, rapidly changing industry situations. But they were able to see that not all uncertain situations were alike—some were more uncertain or were uncertain in different ways. They began to question the common "binary view" of uncertainty—that everything can be determined versus we can know nothing, and instead set about classifying situations by the amount and type of their residual (post-investigation) uncertainty. There are, they contend, four levels of uncertainty:

- Level 1, slow-moving, well-established situations where outcomes are dependable. The prototype of this is the "mature industry," one with a stable set of competitors, not under threat of technology upheavals or regulatory changes, with unchallenged customer segments and supply chains.
- Level 2, where there are a limited and determined set of possible future outcomes, one of which will occur, but we don't know which. This occurs in situations, for example, where there is an impending regulation that may go one way or the other, where a product may be approved or not (e.g., by the FDA), where there may be an industry-changing merger or not, or where different industry technology standards are fighting for adoption.
- Level 3, where outcomes are indeterminate but bounded within a plausible range that can be defined. Implausible or impossible outcomes can be identified and discarded. This type of uncertainty occurs in situations such as those where new products or services are based on new technologies or face uncertain customer demand, or where new delivery models or revenue models are being tried. This type of uncertainty

CHAPTER 7: THE LIMITS OF QUANTITATIVE FORECASTING ◆ 167

is also driven by changes in society, shifting values and norms, or unstable macroeconomic conditions such as oil spikes or currency fluctuations.

- Level 4 refers to very high ambiguity situations where outcomes are unknown and unknowable, and there is a limitless range of possible outcomes. These are situations where new industries—e.g., genomics—are emerging, or where operating conditions are genuinely chaotic and unpredictable due to social or political factors.

The level of uncertainty correlates with the amount of complexity and pace of change in the area under study. It also correlates with the time period under study—the further into the future we look, the higher the uncertainty. The higher the uncertainty level, the more key assumptions are likely to shift over the forecast period.

> *The key insight of the analysis is that each level has analytical tools appropriate to it, and it is futile to use a tool designed for one uncertainty level on a situation or problem that is at another level.*

The key insight of the analysis is that each level has analytical tools appropriate to it, and it is futile to use a tool designed for one uncertainty level on a situation or problem that is at another level. One must match the situation-analysis tools used to the level of uncertainty faced. According to the authors, Level 1 situations are best analyzed with such tools as classic financial valuation (DCF or NPV), Porter's 5-Forces model, standard market research, and other statistical analysis. Level 2 calls for such tools as decision trees or game theory. Among Level 3 tools are scenario planning and real options models. Level 4 has no recognizable analytic tools, but some headway may be made by examining historically analogous situations and using creative visioning tools.

Determining the Right Foresight Approach

Whether one adopts these levels exactly or parses them slightly differently, the basic point remains: We use an analytical tool designed for a low-uncertainty situation in a high-uncertainty situation at our peril.

Low uncertainty forecast situations are ones where:

- There is good and relatively complete data.
- Initial conditions are easy to establish.
- We are dealing with a small, relatively closed system, with few or clear factor inputs, or pairs of closely associated variables rather than many subtly interacting ones.
- The context is relatively static, including stable technologies and stable regulation, and the competitive environment is well understood.
- We are considering a short time horizon.

If, for example, a property consortium wanted to forecast hotel occupancy in the Toronto downtown area for the next five years, it would have quality data about existing occupancies over the past ten years, along with a well-researched picture of tourist promotion business conference initiatives and a thick wad of material from comparable areas of similar size and position. It would be able to come up with a quantitative forecast study that was accurate and helpful in making decisions. Assumptions of cause and effect between variables are likely valid and will remain valid into the five-year future, so the forecast would justifiably be the province of statistics and modeling.

Quantitative forecasting is designed for these situations. Where we have well-known, slow-moving situations with a narrow scope

CHAPTER 7: THE LIMITS OF QUANTITATIVE FORECASTING ♦ 169

> *Factual data is the most objective basis for understanding situations, and a quantitative approach provides a disciplined and objective measure against which we can check our intuitions and experiential judgment.*

and short time frames, it is perfectly possible and reasonable to produce highly valid quantitative forecasts. Not only this, but it is the *best* way forward. As everybody knows, factual data—despite the caveats mentioned in Chapter 2—is the most objective basis for understanding situations, and a quantitative approach provides a disciplined and objective measure against which we can check our intuitions and experiential judgment. It offsets our tendency to be misled by our personal experiences or by focusing on specific cases and immediate situations at the expense of an overall perspective.

Trouble looms, however, when quantitative methods are taken out of low-uncertainty framing conditions. To ask predictive modeling to make medium- or long-term forecasts, or manage other complex, or high-uncertainty future situations—to effectively misread or disregard the uncertainty level—is to invite disaster. As elements and their interaction become less well understood, in situations less bounded and more prone to reversals, number-crunching approaches become less adequate. If the same property consortium was to turn its attention to a fifteen-year future study of hotel occupancy in Havana, the quantitative process that served it well before would now serve it very poorly.

Even as dramatic gains have been made in programming and modeling, no quantitative forecast has ever proved adequate to the task of accurate prediction in high-uncertainty situations or in medium- or long-term situations, and none ever will. Projections fail because they are trying to do the impossible. It is simply beyond us to capture the infinite complexity of possible changes acting in high-uncertainty situations, particularly over the long term. This problem cannot be "solved," not by better forecasting methods, nor better algorithms, nor better computers.

Unfortunately, this does not deter those who quantitatively predict, not least because they are able to hide behind the promise of better software and more powerful computers. Proponents claim that new and ever more sophisticated statistical and data-management and modeling tools, based on ever more powerful computers, will finally make quantitatively based long-term forecasting accurate. Even where a forecast fails miserably, there's always "next time."

Earnest debates about the merits of different modeling methods exist, and each approach has it own proponents and disciples. But, seen from the point of view of appropriateness to uncertainty level, the debate between different models is trivial. Subtly different quantification of the same unsound assumptions will not help. Forecasts that fail are not failing by some small margin that another model would solve. They miss by a mile and would continue to miss if they used a competing model to quantify the future of the same wrong assumptions. As Steven Schnaars (commenting on the utterly failed projections for VTSOL vertical-takeoff aircraft) icily observes, "A fancier version of the same model would have *fallen deeper into the same hole.*"⁹

> Forecasts miss by a mile and would continue to miss if they used a competing model to quantify the future of the same wrong assumptions.

Predictors of man's grand future is space in the twenty-first century, quantitatively projecting metrics of growth in the 1960s, would not have made better predictions if they had more sophisticated models or better computers to run them on. The method of their predictions did not matter, the assumptions did, and those assumptions were dead wrong. As the level of uncertainty we are facing goes up, we must accept that quantitative forecast methods give way to qualitative methods. We help ourselves a lot better by getting approximate answers that are in the right ballpark, rather than exact answers that are not.

Notes

1. Retrieved March 2007 from www.forecastpro.com
2. P. LaPointe, *5 Ways to Better Forecasts* (2006). Retrieved May 2008 from www.dashboardcompany.com
3. Cited in W. Sherden, *The Fortune Sellers* (New York: Wiley & Sons), pp. 197–198.
4. H. Rittel and M. Webber, "Dilemmas in a General Theory of Planning," *Policy Sciences, 4* (1973).
5. M. Gladwell, "Open Secrets," *The New Yorker* (January 8, 2007).
6. *Warfighting: The U.S. Marine Corps Book of Strategy* (New York: Currency Doubleday, 1994).
7. N. Duncan; "Why Can't We Predict?" *New Scientist, 136* (1841) (October 3, 1992), 47.
8. H. Courtney, J. Kirkland, and P. Viguerie "Strategy Under Uncertainty" *Harvard Business Review*, November-December, 1997.
9. S. Schnaars, *Megamistakes* (New York: Free Press, 1989), p. 158.

# CHAPTER 8

A Systems Perspective in Forecasting

WE HAVE SEEN HOW ANTICIPATING THE future often demands interaction with high-complexity, high-uncertainty situations that go beyond where trend extrapolations or quantitative modeling can take us. So how can we approach these situations? There is no perfect tool for this, but systems dynamics, discussed in this chapter, does tackle complex situations head-on and gives us some advantages in anticipating "archetypal" change situations, thus alerting us to forecast errors. In the next chapter we consider scenario planning, a tool for challenging our assumptions and developing nonpredictive views of the future.

Opposite and Side Effects: Introducing Systems

Many human initiatives set out to achieve one goal but end up doing the opposite. Often well-meaning solutions end up exacerbating the problem they are trying to fix. As everyone knows, if you eat a candy bar to remedy low blood sugar, the sugar rush will cause your body to release insulin, leading to even lower blood sugar.[1]

There are many cases that take this form, for example:

- City governments have used residential rent controls to keep housing affordable, yet found this creates additional pressure for rent increases—rent control lowers the return on property investment, which leads to less new building, and a housing shortage puts upward pressure on prices.

- Mandatory use of gloves in professional boxing, meant to make the sport safe, is now considered to have exacerbated long-term, cumulative, chronic brain damage, because it (a) "civilized" boxing, leading to its widespread adoption, and (b) hid the extent of injury, allowing people to box for longer, sometimes a whole career, before the effects became clear.

- Fiscal policymakers have found that raising personal or corporate taxes does not reduce the government budget deficit as hoped, because higher tax rates discourage economic activity, causing aggregate incomes and profits to fall, reducing tax due. (Higher taxes also encourage more tax avoidance and evasion.)

Sometimes initiatives don't create an entirely opposite effect, merely unintended side effects as elements interact in unexpected ways to produce surprising consequences. The most famous example is

CIA funding of militant Islamic opposition to the Soviet Union in Afghanistan in the 1980s, which led to the creation of Al-Qaeda, which threatens the United States. (Military/CIA slang for this kind of unintended and undesirable consequence of operations is, apparently, "blowback.") Another example is 1920s' alcohol prohibition, designed to suppress the alcohol trade, which merely drove smaller suppliers out of the market and consolidated the hold of crime-related conglomerates over the industry.[2]

Whether it is opposite effects or unintended side effects, what we have at work in situations such as these are "system effects," which occur whenever different elements or variables that may appear isolated are in fact linked together such that changes in one element cause secondary changes in others. In other words, when elements are in a system, the particular relationship between any two variables will be determined not just by how they act on each other but also by the influences from other variables in the system. Changing one variable will not only change that variable itself, but also those it is connected to—which is what causes the unexpected or counterintuitive effects. As economists point out, a cut in interest rates makes borrowing more attractive, which stimulates consumer spending, which drives economic growth—but it also drives up inflation, which puts pressure on exchange rates, which exacerbates trade deficits ... so there's no easy fix. No element can be changed without affecting all the others.

> Changing one variable will not only change that variable itself, but also those it is connected to—which is what causes the unexpected or counterintuitive effects.

Anticipating the behavior of a variable that is connected to others in a system hinges on identifying the system's elements and how they relate to each other. The better we understand a system at its structural level, the better we understand how elements in it behave in relation to each other under static conditions, and therefore also how elements are likely to act on each other when a system is subject to forces from the outside.

How Systems Are Modeled

There are many forms of systems modeling, used in different disciplines including engineering and psychology, and they have variously different attributes and goals. The systems approach described here is commonly used for social and economic situations. In these systems, structure is modeled by identifying variables as "stocks," that is *quantities* that can go up or down, and linking them via links or "flows" to show the up-or-down effect of one on another. There are two types of effect. Either two connected variables move in the same direction—one variable going up causes the linked variable to rise too (or a fall leads to a fall), for example, when a rise in factory emissions causes atmospheric CO_2 levels to rise. In the second case, the two variables are connected in opposite directions, that is, one variable going up causes the linked variable to fall (or a fall in one leads to a rise in the other), for example, when a rise in the bank rate dampens the economy or a cut in the bank rate stimulates the economy.

Relationships between variables are plotted as follows:

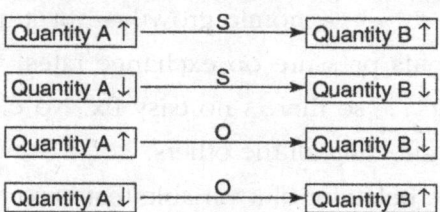

Variables connected with S links: The affected variable goes up or down in the same direction as the stimulating variable. Variables connected with O links: The affected variable moves in the opposite direction.

The affected quantity or stock (B) may then further affect variables that are downstream of it in a causal chain. For example, raising prison sentences for drug pushers causes the supply of drugs to fall, which raises the price, which makes them more attractive to farm and produce.

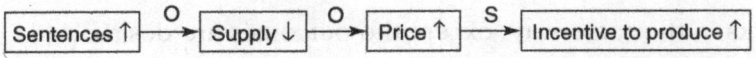

In this way, a chain of causality can be represented. The key thing that defines a systems perspective—and separates a systems model from a flow chart—is that it seeks places where the chain of causality returns to affect the original variable, that is, where a closed or "feedback" loop appears. In the example above, raised incentive to produce drugs will raise supply on the streets, which will lead to more public concern, which will lead to more pressure on lawmakers, which will lead to stricter sentencing, closing the loop.

Reinforcing Loops: Vicious and Virtuous Cycles

A closed loop will have either a reinforcing or balancing effect depending on the nature of its links. A reinforcing loop occurs where change in one variable affects others in a loop such that the chain of causality returns to affect the original variable in the *same* direction. For example, a company that is losing money may cut corners on product quality, which leads to inferior products, which leads to customer dissatisfaction, which leads to customers switching to a competitor's product, which leads to the

> *A reinforcing loop occurs where change in one variable affects others in a loop such that the chain of causality returns to affect the original variable in the* same *direction.*

company's losing more money (the original variable), which leads the company to further cut corners on product quality, and so on. In this case, the initial downward shift—the company's losing money—is reinforced or amplified by the system it is part of. Losing money causes the company to lose even more money, in a situation commonly known as a "vicious cycle." A virtuous cycle works in the same way, except the outcomes are desirable.

Reinforcing cycles are associated with growth or decline, and particularly, exponential growth or decline. Through reinforcing feedback, the system renews a change and magnifies its effect. Thus, even a small initial change, when amplified through a constantly reinforcing loop creates an exponential or "epidemic" effect, which results in a surprisingly significant—and often unforeseen—ultimate effect.

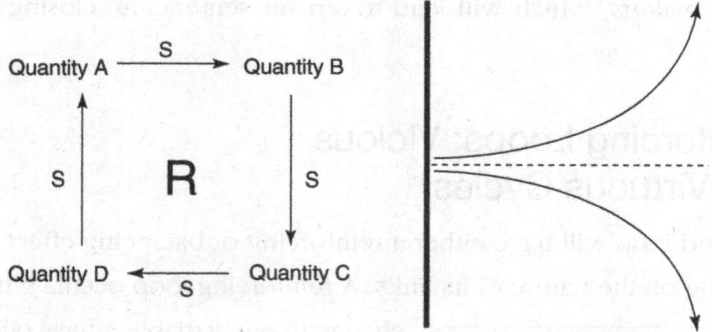

Reinforcing loops are associated with exponential behavior and change.

Balancing Loops: The Change Dampers

In contrast to a reinforcing loop, a "balancing" loop is one where the system responds in the *opposite* direction to the initial change—which feeds back to dampen or nullify the initial change.[3] This is sometimes called "negative" or stabilizing feedback. The system ef-

> A "balancing" loop is one where the system responds in the opposite direction to the initial change—which feeds back to dampen or nullify the initial change.

fectively reasserts initial-state conditions and will keep variables at a mean point or (if delays are present) oscillating around it. A thermostat control system makes use of balancing feedback: The system is set to respond in the opposite direction to the temperature, that is, as temperature falls, the heat comes on and vice versa.

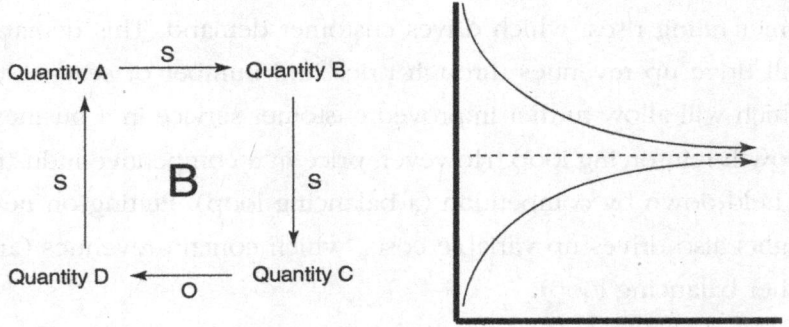

Balancing loops are associated with stable, self-correcting, or "goal-seeking" behavior.

As reinforcing feedback creates conditions of exponential change, balancing feedback creates conditions of stasis and equilibrium. A system dominated by a reinforcing loop will exhibit exponential growth or decline in values of key variables. A system dominated by a balancing loop will be more or less stable and will remain there unless it is acted on by a force of change that overcomes the balancing mechanism.

Charting Multiple Simultaneous Causes and Effects

Each variable in a system will have many variables affecting it, and it in turn may affect many others, so full system modeling becomes quite complex. And this is very much the point—to be able to understand the system in such a way that as many elements and their simultaneous interactions as possible are represented and accounted for, rather than projecting one element while wishing the others away. The total picture is represented with a systems diagram, also known as a causal loop diagram, which shows many stocks, flows, and feedback loops.

By way of example, the diagram below is a high-level systems view of the situations airline companies are in. It tells us that as an airline raises its offering via better aircraft or service quality, its customer rating rises, which drives customer demand. This demand will drive up revenues through price and number of seats sold, which will allow further improved customer service in a business growth reinforcing loop. However, price in a competitive industry is held down by competition (a balancing loop). Putting on new flights also drives up variable costs, which contain revenues (another balancing loop).

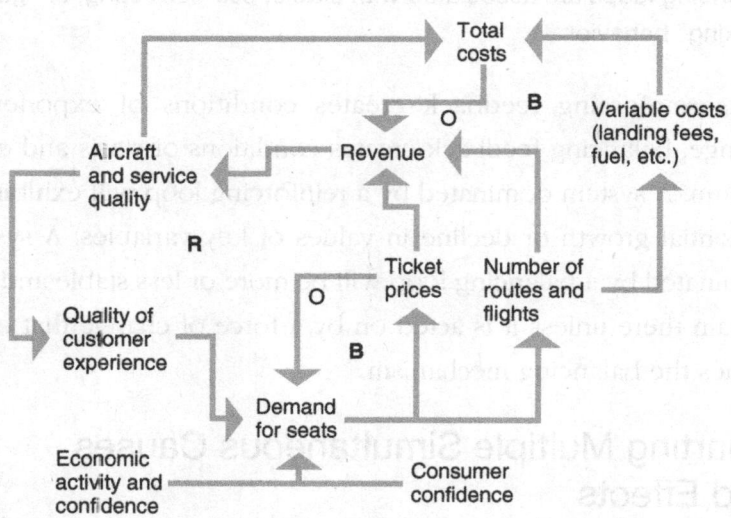

A high-level systems diagram of the system an airline company finds itself in, illustrating reinforcing (R) and balancing (B) loops. (All links S unless marked).

The system builder can choose to view the system at a higher level, which promotes high-level perspective, or a more detailed level (with all subsystems charted), which promotes granularity of explanation. No system is a perfect representation of reality, of course, and different analysts may see the relationships between elements differently.

Causal Loop Diagrams Are Nonpredictive

It is beyond the scope of this book to discuss causal loop diagrams in any detail. The intention is merely to extract the value in this approach for filtering and evaluating forecasts, showing how it allows us to spot common situations and dismiss common errors in forecasting, as discussed below. But first, it is important to realize that systems models are not in themselves predictive. A causal loop model tells us nothing about the future, for many reasons. No forces or blockers of change are accounted for. It does not specify initial data points, and although causal loop models try to incorporate all elements of change, there is no guarantee that all factors are there or that the links accurately depict present, let alone future, reality. Also, the nature of their connections is highly simplified. In the terms discussed in the previous chapter, we don't know the lag, thresholds, or shape (mathematical form of the relationship, assuming it is not always 1-to-1) that exist in a flow from one variable to another.

> A causal loop model tells us nothing about the future, for many reasons.

Some attempts to quantify systems dynamics and make it a predictive tool have been made, notably through *Stella* software, but it meets with success only where there is good and relatively complete data, where initial conditions are easy to establish, and we are dealing with a small, relatively closed system with few or clear factor inputs and a short time horizon—the conditions for success that apply to all quantitative forecasting.

However, charting elements and feedback loops does give us insight into the causal structure that underpins a situation under study, and therefore gives us a powerful way to assess the anticipated effects of a change or judge a forecast of change. First, a causal loop diagram shows us the folly, if any more convincing was necessary, in making single-issue or single-trend predictions. There is no element that is not systemically connected to others and therefore subject to broader systemic effects. When change acts on an element we are interested in forecasting, it is acting on the whole system. This shows why we cannot assume that a change will have its intended effect, and therefore why we cannot confidently forecast that effect. Feedback may turn an apparently straightforward influence into an unexpected change, or no change at all. While it is sometimes unclear which loops will prevail, their existence primes us to see that some outside forces will have zero effect (where balancing forces dominate) or have disproportionate and rapid effect (where reinforcing forces dominate). With this in mind, a good forecast will direct attention as to how the system as a whole will respond to any new stimulus rather than assuming a simple straight-line cause-and-effect world.

> A good forecast will direct attention as to how the system as a whole will respond to any new stimulus rather than assuming a simple straight-line cause-and-effect world.

Understanding the systemic structure behind observed events also helps us avoid further common thinking (and forecasting) traps and better evaluate what others predict, as detailed in the following sections.

Anticipating Systemic Effects on Personal Behavior

A systems perspective encourages focus on structural reasons for behavior, and therefore to avoid personalizing explanations unnecessarily. We often think things happen because particular people make them happen or that we would get different outcomes if there were different people involved. "If that country was to overthrow its leader, or if that company would find new suppliers, or if the workers at our factory were more like foreign workers, etc., then we'd see (a new future)." People are important, and particular personalities do shape events, but the systems perspective allows us to balance this with a knowledge that, often, if one replaces a person or group of people, one does not change outcomes. An employee will behave like an employee and a boss will behave like a boss, no matter which person is in those roles, because of the systemic incentive patterns that surround them. It is less the personality or nature of the protagonist and more the intrinsic dynamics of the system that shapes actions.[4]

If some agency were, for example, able to change the president of Zimbabwe, the chances are the next incumbent—even if excellent—would still be beset by Shona versus Matebele tribal rifts, civil service corruption, failure of the Zimbabwe dollar, and so on, and hopes for a better future would be frustrated by these systemic elements. The new incumbent might have political debts to pay or might need to consolidate power against unsavory opponents, which might exacerbate corruption and mismanagement, and spending on armaments rather than food, and so reinforce the elements that create the problem.

If personal behavior is highly determined by the system that actions play out in, this means that it is better to base explanations of present and future behavior on systemic structure—the relationship and interaction of a system's constituent parts—than on any person's or any organization's particular "nature." The corollary is, obviously, if we see a change in how a system is structured—how it functions and how elements relate to each other—we should expect changes in actors' behavior.

Anticipating Critical Mass and Tipping Points

Seeing systems at work helps us anticipate "tipping points" that mark the beginning of rapid change. The tipping point is the point where a reinforcing loop is sprung into action. Due to a new technology or change in regulation or new consumer demand, for example, a threshold is crossed or critical mass is reached—meaning one variable in a reinforcing loop becomes raised, causing all the others to be raised via feedback, in a reinforcing spiral that overpowers the balancing loops that are keeping the situation in stasis. If we can see such conditions favoring a reinforcing loop becoming dominant, we should forecast significant growth (or decline) in the key variable.

> The tipping point is the point where a reinforcing loop is sprung into action.

For example, it could be anticipated that digital photography would follow a path to the future that followed the shape of slow emergence, a tipping point, and exponential growth. The technology was developed in the 1980s, and the first digital cameras were available in the early 1990s, but for most of that decade less than 2% of photographers were using digital cameras. Over time the technology improved, got smaller, lighter, cheaper, and more reliable, producing sharper pictures using less memory. At the same time, other forces were moving in its favor in the broader system, particularly the widespread adoption of home computers, mobile phones, and the evolution of online peer-to-peer communication and social networking. In the early 2000s, a tipping point was reached where the comparative benefits of digital photography were incontrovertible, due to both technology advances and interactivity with the rest of the digital world. As mass adoption occurred, so more occurred, in a reinforcing spiral. Note that, in the terms discussed in Chapter 5, adoption followed a rise in total utility. More adoption allows greater economies of scale in production, which lowers unit cost, raises utility, and further stimulates adoption.[5]

In this case, reinforcing exponential growth behavior was also due to what is known as "network effects," which occur when adoption itself makes a product more attractive. As the famous example goes, one fax machine in the world is useless; two fax machines are mostly useless; but as more people get fax machines they became more and more useful, leading more people and companies to acquire them (following positive utility), making them even more useful in a reinforcing way. This is true of services as well. The more members an online dating site has, for example, the more attractive it becomes, and the faster new members sign up, creating exponential adoption.

Anticipating Forecasts Designed to Stimulate a Virtuous Cycle

An exponential growth feedback loop is, of course, the desire of business decision makers. The basic business virtuous growth cycle is investment to achieve a unique advantage in products or services, which leads to pricing power, which lead to profits, which allows (after some profits returned to investors) further investment, leading to further unique advantages, and so on. Exponential growth is similarly sought in the social and policy sphere. An inner-city administration may try, for example, to fundraise to develop good schools, which would attract middle-class residents, which would raise property prices, which would raise the local tax base, which would allow further development of good schools (and other benefits.)

As a virtuous growth cycle is a good thing to have, business leaders or policy makers often set about trying to talk a virtuous cycle into being by predicting it—that is, making a future-influencing prediction designed to take a reinforcing loop to its tipping point, after which it will grow under its own steam. These forecasters are using a forecast to stimulate the growth prospects of feedback loop, rather than trying to make an accurate prediction. Epidemic adoption is particularly the holy grail for marketers who try to create enough adoption through advertising and other forms of marketing to push a product to critical mass. If movie marketers, for example, say a new movie is "sure to be the smash hit of the summer," this is not their real best guess. They are trying to raise consumer interest enough so that more people will see the movie, such that there will be enough talk about it, so that more will see it, in a reinforcing loop that will ultimately make the movie a box-office success.

Anticipating S-Curves and the Limits of Change

> *Eventually, a threshold is reached where balancing forces—usually market or resource or physical or capacity saturation—assert themselves, meaning that the period of acceleration is followed by deceleration, and key variables will eventually reach equilibrium.*

A systems perspective will allow us to see that while powerful reinforcing loops leading to exponential change conditions may exist for a significant time, they won't exist indefinitely. Eventually, a threshold is reached where balancing forces—usually market or resource or physical or capacity saturation—assert themselves, meaning that the period of acceleration is followed by deceleration, and key variables will eventually reach equilibrium. The system returns to balance, albeit at a new position.

Reinforcing behavior followed by balancing behavior makes up the familiar S-curve of change. In the early phase, a reinforcing loop dominates, and there is exponential growth (or decline) in behavior of the key variable. In later stages, balancing loops prevail and return the system to equilibrium. For example, as diagrammed below, in a typical market entry, a sales force will be hired to sell a new product. Assuming the product is good and the market ready, sales will go through a reinforcing loop: Higher sales lead to higher commission income, which raises morale, which raises productivity, which leads to higher sales, and so on. (Other reinforcing feedback loops will drive sales, for example, sales of a good product will lead to satisfied customers, which will increase word-of-mouth advertising, which will drive sales.) But after a while, the market will become saturated, or competition will emerge, and this will dampen sales income. These balancing forces will ultimately smother further change and cause the curve to flatten.

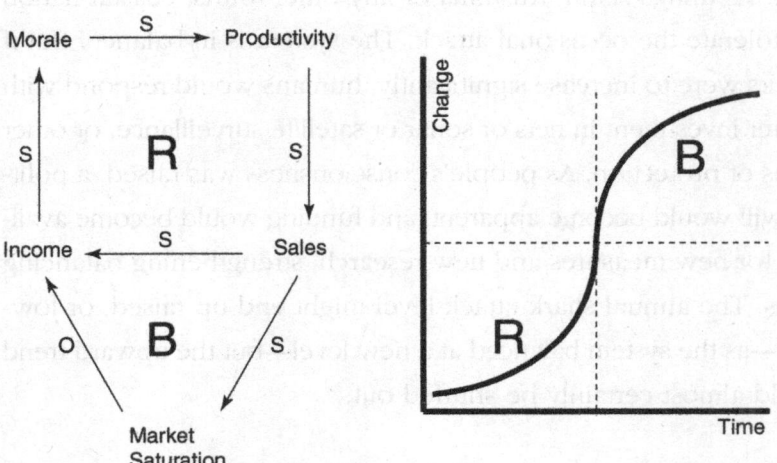

S-curve changes occur when reinforcing system effects dominate, but are ultimately overcome by balancing systemic effects.

The wisdom of S-curves shows us that change happens between two more-or-less stable equilibrium states. Change is a move from one equilibrium point to another, and the trend we witness is that movement. Once a new equilibrium point is reached, the change stops. In the terms defined in the Chapter 6, systems at balance have powerful blockers in place.

The naïve forecast would see a growth trend and project it forward without considering what balancing loops exist or at what threshold balancing forces will assert themselves to dissipate the change. For example, if sharks, deprived of natural habitat and food sources due to global warming, were to start attacking people in greater numbers off Australia's Gold Coast, we might see the number of attacks triple in three years. It would appear that attacks are on a consistent upward curve, and we may be inclined to project the current growth trend to make a prediction of more frequent attacks in five years, and even more in ten years. This would be nonsense because it would not account for systemic feedback. As things stand, Australia or any other tourist coastal nation can tolerate the occasional attack. The system is in balance. But if attacks were to increase significantly, humans would respond with greater investment in nets or sonar or satellite surveillance, or other forms of protection. As people's consciousness was raised, a political will would become apparent, and funding would become available for new measures and new research, strengthening balancing loops. The annual shark attack level might end up raised, or lowered—as the system balanced at a new level—but the upward trend would almost certainly be snuffed out.

Anticipating Accelerations or Delays

The systems perspective shows why considering cause and effect on one variable on its own leads us to an incorrect, usually overoptimistic, view of how long a change will take. Such a forecasting error often occurs in the honeymoon phase of a business or product emergence, when change is exponential. Some will project this forward, projecting the current pace of change, only to be proved wrong when the change slows. A systems view shows us that it is most unlikely that a trend will move at the same rate through its life cycle and how we may expect delays or accelerations as the system digests and responds to a stimulus. In an S-curve change, for example, there are times where change moves quickly and times when it slows dramatically. If we were to consider the emergence of the electronic book, for example, it would be tempting to take the rate at which electronic books are currently being made or bought, or the number of texts created for electronic books, or any other related metric, and extrapolate that (currently slow) rate of change. But it would be wrong. What is more likely to happen is systemic effect leading to a long incubation period of slow change followed by accelerated adoption before the trend slows again.

Anticipating Oscillations and Pendulum Swings

In a system that is strongly at balance, changes may not be balanced at a new equilibrium point (the S-curve) but reversed so strongly that they unravel entirely. In these cases change will either reach a maximum point and then unwind completely to revert to the status quo or oscillate around a mean point. This can be seen, for example, in election success for conservative versus liberal governments—after a spell of conservativism, the liberals will get in, and after a spell of liberal government, it's back to the conservatives. This often mirrors other pendulum swings in society, as the level of religiosity or social permissiveness swings one way and then the other. Sometimes, the pendulum takes generations or more to go through the full cycle. Atomic energy was all the rage in the

1950s and so popular that people were predicting atomic cars and atomic vacuum cleaners. But by the 1980s, after the Three-Mile Island and Chernobyl incidents, the technology was a political and social dead duck. Forecasts at that time showed nuclear energy disappearing as soon as power plants reached the end of their lives. But in the early twenty-first century, in an era of growing global energy needs, and concern over carbon emissions and over the politics of oil supply, nuclear energy has returned as a mainstream technology. A systemic view helps us avoid the mistake of seeing one side of a pendulum move and forecasting a changed world where in fact forces are such that the pendulum will eventually swing the other way.

Questioning the "Exponential Change" View

Balancing loops, and their manifestation in S-curve and pendulum effects, help us overcome a common myth about change that bedevils forecasting—that our world is changing at an "exponential" rate. While we may experience "future shock" in response to change around us, and it often feels as though we are living in a unique era of unprecedented change and that "time is speeding up," this perception does not stand up to logical or empirical analysis and is part of a low-quality world view that causes errors in forecasting.

It is true that the world has seen new products and services and lifestyles rapidly drive out old standards and traditions particularly through transformation to information and communication technologies in the past twenty-five years. And these advances have yet to combine fully with other emerging technologies, principally bio- and nanotechnologies, that appear likely to allow us to build materials and engines at the atomic level, and even to take control of life itself and create synthetic life. Brain sciences promise transformational enhancements in human cognition, and genuine artificial intelligence, among other things. However, these expected innovations and many others still do not mean that we are or will be experiencing more or faster change than that experienced in previous eras.

Over the past two centuries change has been at least as rapid and profound as the world changed to accommodate the steam engine, railways, the automobile, airplanes, electricity, refrigeration, anesthesia, vaccines, antibiotics, X-rays, steel, concrete, the telephone, radio, movies, etc. Not only were these various new technologies and capabilities every bit as disorienting as we face today, but they were also as profound. The need for railway schedules led to the first standardization of time. The needs of industry led to humans becoming primarily city and metropolitan dwellers in the past century, after being village and rural dwellers since the dawn of humanity. Early communications technologies created new mass industries in the media and entertainment. Contraceptive power over reproduction has allowed new roles for women, which has led to profound social change in work and home life.

> This is to say that it is in fact very likely—if one could adequately judge such a measure—that on most fronts we are experiencing less *future shock* now than people 100 years ago.

This is to say that it is in fact very likely—if one could adequately judge such a measure—that on most fronts we are experiencing *less* future shock now than people 100 years ago. We are able to get fancy refrigerators that will warn us when food is going bad, but this does not compare with the original innovation of domestic and commercial refrigeration that fundamentally changed how kitchens or shopping were organized, and which created and broke whole industries (ice cutting and ice-transport shipping disappeared). Similarly, there may be innovations in noninvasive and microsurgery, but does this compare with anesthesia for change value? We are amazed we can reach anyone at any time on their cell phone, but this is no more amazing than the telegraph that replaced stage coaches and smoke signals. We think we are at the fastest, most fundamentally disorienting moment in history, but people thought this in 1850, too, and in 1950, and had at least as much cause to.

So while the transitions we face in the early twenty-first century certainly involve constant, rapid change, they are not unique in terms of pace, scale, or reach, and there is nothing to suggest change is faster and more pervasive than before, or that it is speeding up. It is possible—probable even—that in new areas such a biotechnology or nanotechnology, change will be exponential for a while as discoveries are made and myriad product opportunities found, just as previous technologies also had their exponential period. But this will soon pass. As a systems view suggests, the "exponential change" view of the future is invalid, and forecasts based on this view will overestimate change. Understanding the balancing forces at work in all the systems around us helps us reign in and reality-test forecasts that are premised on this fallacy.

> As a systems view suggests, the "exponential change" view of the future is invalid, and forecasts based on this view will overestimate change.

Notes

1. Systems are ubiquitous—all human and natural phenomena are arranged in interconnected systems. A system can be a physical entity, such as the solar system; or an ecological system, such as a forest; a biological system, such as the human body; or a social system, such as a family or a neighborhood.

2. Examples cited in S. Walt, "The Hidden Nature of Systems," *The Atlantic Monthly* (September 1998).
3. If the loop has one O link, or any odd number of O links, it will be a balancing loop.
4. This is sometimes also called "fundamental attribution error," referring to the human tendency to overemphasize personality-based explanations for behavior, while underemphasizing the role of situational influences.
5. The way exponential product adoption or diffusion works through a reinforcing cycle is defined by Everett Rogers. In the beginning there are few people ("innovators") involved with an innovation—too few to assuage the doubts of the majority. Very slow growth happens. However, as the innovation gains good reputation (including among key opinion leaders), more people will adopt it, leading to a tipping point at around the "early adopter" or "early majority" stage. Most who will adopt an innovation at all adopt rapidly after this point. E. Rogers, *Diffusion of Innovations* (New York: Free Press, 1962).

CHAPTER 9

Alternative Futures:
How It's Better
to Be Vaguely
Right than
Exactly Wrong

IN PREVIOUS CHAPTERS WE HAVE DEALT WITH THE pros and cons of predictive approaches to anticipating the future and showed why forecasters are in over their heads attempting to predict accurately in situations where uncertainty and complexity are high or when systemic feedback creates unexpected effects. The shameful record of many absurdly wrong forecasts speaks for itself. Point predictions fail in many situations, and as they do, other approaches become necessary.

Redefining Forecast Expectations

Forecasting "alternative futures," the mantra of qualitative, judgmental forecasting, takes its raison d'etre from the shortcomings of all forecasting methods that aim to come up with an exact future prediction. It approaches the problem by turning the goal of forecasting on its head. If the world is too complex for anyone or any computer to hit the mark perfectly, why even try? It revisits the question of what we are aiming to achieve in the first place, and asks, How "right" do we need to be? After all, the real goal of forecasting is not to predict the future. This is just an interim step en route to the actual goal, which is to achieve future success.

> *So, the question becomes: How right does a forecast need to be to be useful in helping us making good decisions toward future success? The test of a good forecast is not the classic question: "Is it correct?"*

So, the question becomes: How right does a forecast need to be to be useful in helping us making good decisions toward future success? The test of a good forecast is not the classic question: "Is it correct?" It is the utilitarian question: "Is it useful in producing success?" In a world where prediction is impossible, but the future is important, the alternative futures perspective says forecasts are valid and useful if they alert us to a situation that is changing in important ways, and prepare us or our organizations for those changes within a future that remains uncertain. We can't know if a forecast will be correct—and chances are it will not be—so even a forecast that turns out to be dead right may, ironically, not stimulate a necessary action response because nobody would plan for its being right. On the other hand, the forecast that gets us thinking, asking the right questions, challenging our assumptions, and illuminating choices may stimulate a better response, which leads to the right decisions and so is highly useful even if many of its details about the future are wrong.

This nontraditional attitude about forecasts opens up a new concept of forecast practice—one that is more about managing uncertainty than predicting the future. It acknowledges unfathomable complexity of the world by "giving in" and identifying possible alternatives. This is a circumspect and modest definition, and in some senses recasts our expectations downwards. The goal is not to predict anything, but to think about the future in a broad way, and by so doing gain insight into the capabilities and strategies that help us determine robust solutions that will succeed in an inherently uncertain future. By shining a light on uncertainty, without predicting its resolutions, or burying complexity and hoping it goes away, decision makers promote their mental and organizational readiness for whatever the future does bring.

Scenarios:
Thinking the Unthinkable

The key qualitative forecasting method based on alternative futures is scenario planning (also known as "scenario building"). Like many management techniques, scenarios have come to industry from the military. As the story goes, scenarios emerged into business and policy forecasting from the work of Herman Kahn, a *Rand Corporation* analyst in the 1950s who, apparently influenced by screenwriters and moviemakers of Los Angeles of that time, including Stanley Kubrick, started "telling stories" about how nuclear war might emerge and play out. By the mid-1960s, Kahn was producing dozens of alternative story forecasts. Each scenario followed different key assumptions to its logical conclusion. He was branded by *Scientific American* as "thinking the unthinkable," a soundbite that has been proudly worn by scenario planners ever since.

Kahn's work attracted a visit from Pierre Wack, Head of Planning at *Royal Dutch/ Shell*, France. Using and further developing the approach at Shell, Wack and his co-workers produced, in 1971, various scenarios for the oil industry, each based on different assumptions about how key uncertainties would resolve. As reported by Wack in a series of *Harvard Business Review* articles, at the time it was generally sensed that geopolitical change, particularly the rise of Arab nationalism, would change the status quo in the oil industry, which Western oil companies had dominated for decades.[1] In what is now the legendary story of scenario planning success, Shell forced itself to confront then-seemingly outrageous scenario of an oil supply shock, where the oil price rose rapidly. In the event, this is more or less what happened after the Yom Kippur War in 1973 and again during the Iranian revolution of 1979.

Although Shell had not planned exclusively for a supply shock, nor predicted it, it was nevertheless able to respond more quickly and effectively than its competitors, returning better results and dramatically improving its industry position over the decade and beyond.[2] The supply shock scenario achieved the management thinking breakthrough the company needed by reversing a then-key current assumption (oil price stability), which allowed planners to make visible a train of future outcomes that were otherwise difficult if not impossible to see within the current industry paradigm. In doing this, they prepared themselves to see, understand, and respond, if and when they entered a future that had elements of a supply shock scenario.

Through stories such as these, scenario planning gained proponents inside and outside of business planning and has steadily gained currency worldwide in business, government, military, civic, and policy planning since the 1980s. At this time many corporations had classic old-style strategic planning departments that were synonymous with data-driven quantitative, predictive forecasting, and therefore with forecast error. Famously, one of the first things Jack Welch did on taking the reins at GE was to close its strategic planning department, a fate suffered by many similar departments due to frustration at an all-too-apparent inability to look ahead accurately despite vast resources thrown at the problem.

Tackling Assumptions: Breaking Free of the "Official Future"

Scenarios are built around identifying and reversing an organization's most important assumptions in this way. Building forecasting around alternative assumptions forces scenario planners to break out of their standard worldview or commonly accepted view of the future, sometimes known as the "official future." None of the scenarios is a prediction. In fact, no scenario in a set is meant to stand alone. They exist in sets—normally between two and four in a set—each with different structuring assumptions—that is, a different underlying theory about the future—presenting a different "argument," prioritizing certain actors or forces in the future, to create a different interpretation of the way present uncertainties will move to resolution.

> Building forecasting around alternative assumptions forces scenario planners to break out of their standard worldview or commonly accepted view of the future, sometimes known as the "official future."

Between them the set covers the spectrum of different ways that important uncertainties might play out. Taken together, they outline the terrain of plausible uncertainty that is important for the organization going forward and explore of the credible and important range of future conditions, possibilities, opportunities, threats, and obstacles in alternative future environments, in which decisions taken today may be played out.[3] When done properly, they are different enough to the official future, and to each other, to force acknowledgment of opportunities or challenges that are not part of everyday planning and allow decision makers to consider discontinuities and so get thinking what their challenges and best options will be in each case. In this way the future—even while it is not predicted—is mentally rehearsed along a number of alternative dimensions. Through this rehearsal, decision makers also become mentally prepared to recognize the direction the future is taking while it is unfolding, therein avoiding surprises, adapting more quickly, and making better decisions.

In his book *The Living Company*,[4] another Shell planning executive, Arie de Geus, describes how scenario planning turns conventional predictive forecasting and predict-and-control planning on its head. The future-thinking process is no longer about spending time and energy determining what the most likely outcome is, and planning for it, but assuming every important different plausible outcome is possible (including, where relevant, wildcard events) and considering how the organization should respond. Rather than investing resources to accurately predict what will happen—a futile task—scenario-based management just assumes that every important outcome does happen and then asks, "What would we do if X happened?" "What would we do if Y happened?" And so on.

In this way, scenarios are constructed around "what if . . . ?" questions about the ways in which external forces may emerge to impact the organization. An oil supply shock was not Shell's "prediction." It was neither what forecasters thought was going to happen, nor what they thought was most likely to happen. It was what they thought *might* happen—merely one of various alternative resolutions of the uncertainty picture that they considered.

> Part of the power of scenarios is that they mimic how most people mentally deal with future uncertainty and change in their lives.

Part of the power of scenarios is that they mimic how most people mentally deal with future uncertainty and change in their lives. When we consider a job in a new city, for example, we think of where this will take us in our career, what doors will be opened and what doors closed. We think how it might affect our family and friendships. This is a scenario. Then we consider how things would evolve if we don't take it—another scenario. As we think ahead, we run alternative future scenarios in our heads, intuitively prethinking how the world will play out in various scenarios and considering our ability to reach our desires or goals in each scenario.

Creating Scenarios

Business and industry scenarios typically look five to fifteen years ahead. In policy fields, there may be call to consider longer terms— for example, a civic authority may think thirty years ahead when designing an urban environment and setting up an urban transport system. Military planners may also often have the luxury of looking deep into the future. After deciding on the foresight length relevant to the organization, scenario planning begins with gathering information and insight through a variety of horizon-scanning and trend-tracking methods, looking at industry and social data and changing technologies to get a overall sense of the changes affecting the environment the organization must perform in.

Once this information is assembled, the scenario-building process separates changes into *predetermined elements* and *critical uncertainties*. Predetermined elements are outcomes that are considered to be certain over the time frame of the scenarios and will lead to outcomes that can be relied on—for example, a locked-in degree of income disparity, predictable cuts in public spending, or a demographic shift may be considered predetermined. Wack compared predetermined elements to predictions of floods on the Ganges River: If you see that monsoon rains have occurred in the upper basin in the Himalayas, you know with certainty that within a few days, floods will occur lower down, and with experience you can predict where the flood is going to be. Predetermined elements describe "the known future implications of something that has already happened."[5] If an element is considered predetermined, it will, by definition, feature or be implied in every scenario.

Uncertainties, on the other hand, are the potential changes that scenario builders are unsure about—unsure either about the direction of change or the resulting outcome or the pace of evolution. Uncertainties are outcomes that could resolve various ways, or any of a number of ways—and we don't and can't know which way or when. (Uncertainties here mean uncertainties in the world that the organization has no control over, not its own choices where it may be uncertain what to do.) Because scenario makers don't know how these uncertainties will resolve, and don't pretend that they know or even should know, they explore the various alternatives. They make an assumption about how a key uncertainty will resolve and explore that, and then reverse it or explore other assumptions, each resulting in a different story about how the future resolves. For example, in a situation where an organization does not know whether it is facing an industry-wide move to a new mobile technology standard and also expects significant legislation in its industry but is unsure what will emerge and how long it will take, it may assume the new standard occurs within a lax legislative environment, which it calls Scenario 1. Then it may assume the standard emerges in a stiff legislative environment and calls that Scenario 2. Then it may assume the standard doesn't occur but the legislation does, in Scenario 3, and so on.

> In this way scenarios taken together explore the "cone of plausible uncertainty," that is, the area where events are plausible yet uncertain.

In this way scenarios taken together explore the "cone of plausible uncertainty," that is, the area where events are plausible yet uncertain. Plausibility is normally set wide—the point is to see unexpected events or "wildcards." But outcomes that are judged to fail the plausibility test remain

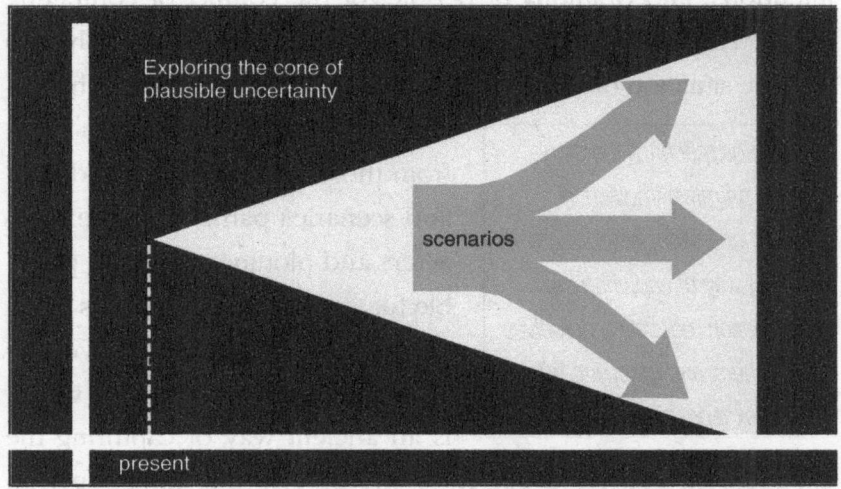

Scenarios together explore alternative plausible outcomes, based on different assumptions about how important uncertainties will resolve.

outside the limit of standard business and policy scenario planning.

If scenarios are well constructed, they are put through a number of internal tests to verify their logic and assess whether each scenario's events would credibly happen, asking if there is convincing utility gain for the most powerful players or whether the scenario accounts for the impact of powerful systemic blockers, including opposing stakeholders who would respond in a contrary way. In this way, the organization will investigate a set of distinct alternative plausible ways uncertainties outside of its control may evolve from the present and come together to change the environment it will be required to operate in.

Data and Narrative

Good scenarios are based on good data and contain alternative visions of how the data moves forward. But scenarios are designed to go past a number-bound perspective, to also capture the interests, intentions, and opinions of people, or the conflict of competing forces. They are, above all, *stories* about how the world evolves to a future situation or snapshots of what it would look like in that situation. The term "scenario" is taken from the world of theater and film, and scenarios particularly use characters and plotlines to evoke possible future situations. Scenarios reach for the storytelling, narrative tradition in human cognition, which is an ancient way of capturing the imagination, educating ourselves and others, and grappling with complex tapestry of life.

> Scenarios reach for the storytelling narrative tradition in human cognition, which is an ancient way of capturing the imagination, educating ourselves and others, and grappling with complex tapestry of life.

As organizational storytelling evangelist Steve Denning says, "Analytic, abstract thinking is ideal for reporting the regular, the expected, the normal, the ordinary. . . . By contrast, narrative thinking, encapsulated in stories and storytelling, is ideally suited to discussing the exceptional. Narrative thrives on the disruptions from the ordinary, the unexpected, the conflicts, the deviations, the surprises, the unusual. Stories flourish in the overthrow of the existing order by some event or thought that changes our perspective."[6] In this way, scenarios search for an "aha effect" that occurs when managers see a new threat or possibility, or a new strategy—an insight that can be lost amid a thousand spreadsheets.

Scenarios as Strategy Testbeds

As we have seen, scenario planning changes the goal of forecasting, from determining the future, to seeing important alternative plausible outcomes, and each scenario is an alternative, plausible, future—a model future world—that implies different operating circumstances that managers may have to adapt to or navigate through to reach their goals. In the terms of scenario planner Kees van der Heijden, scenarios are therefore "testbeds" or wind tunnels for management decisions, be they business or policy decisions.[7] If we understand the challenges and opportunities that a particular operating environment would present, we can test planned actions against the different conditions these scenarios present—for example, asking, How does our current strategy hold up in each scenario? Will it provide the necessary elements of success in that scenario? Alternatively, we can look at the scenario and ask, What will the necessary key capabilities be? What is the organization's present strength in these capabilities? In this way we can test current (or alternative) strategies against a number of different model worlds, to see what actions, products, resources, skills, etc., will be needed in any of the scenarios, and thus prepare robustly to be viable and competitive whatever comes to pass.

Clearly, there is redundancy in preparing for multiple scenarios—what is a best strategy for one scenario may be different from what is required for another. In fact, the two may be incompatible. Scenarios do not resolve this conflict, they merely illuminate it and challenge an organization to be prepared for alternative outcomes, with appropriately resilient strategies. After that, sometimes management just has to make choices and lay their bets (and set contingent strategies or hedges). It is tempting to try to pick which scenario is most likely—for example, by assigning probability to each one, and then planning for the most likely one. This would mean returning to a predictive forecasting with its attendant problems. In fact, if there is one most likely scenario, this means that the scenarios have been badly constructed. Properly done, all scenarios should appear more or less equally plausible and of equally serious consequence to the organization. (Note that scenarios are always pictures of events external to the organization. Planners may then, on the back of these, create "strategy scenarios"—choosing to think what actions they would take and how they would play out in each scenario.)

Visionary Scenarios

As scenario planning has come into the foresight mainstream, it is no surprise that the method has been adopted by both future-aligning and future-influencing forecasters, as defined in Chapter 1. Future-aligners aim to create a set of scenarios that broadly captures the spectrum of plausible outcomes. Future-influencers create scenarios that look like these in many ways, and share many of the same elements, but have a different purpose. As we've seen, the point of future-influencers is to change the world. Therefore, these scenarios are created in such a way that one outcome is very much preferable (the utopia or vision), and it is compared to other scenarios that sketch the less good or awful future outcomes (the muddle-through scenarios and the dystopia). Oftentimes, the dystopia is all that is communicated, as in, for example, a global warming scenario, with the implication that we need to change our actions to avoid this scenario's becoming the future.

A famous set of visionary scenarios were created during the transition in South Africa where the *Flight of the Flamingos* vision was written as an evocative story of what a "best outcome" would look like.[8] The variously less good and terrible *Lame-Duck*, *Icarus*, and *Ostrich* scenario outcomes were placed alongside the vision to show what might happen if the right choices were not made. These scenarios, as with all visionary scenarios, were made to be widely publicized and asked the forecast consumer to help make changes in the world for a better future. The point of the exercise was to communicate the vision to white and black hardliners and get them to change their demands and their behavior, for the good of all. In contrast, future-anticipators, making anticipatory scenarios, use scenarios in a much more "agnostic" way.

They are tasking themselves to explore future possibilities, to be ready for whatever occurs. Some outcomes are better, of course, but no outcome is necessarily to be preferred. The point is to be ready for whatever occurs. Anticipatory scenarios are typically company confidential.

The Limits of Scenarios

The scenario approach is important for the purpose of forecast filtering because it shows what can and should be done when situations are too complex to be knowable or predictable in any exact way. Scenarios provide a challenge to the conventional model of what a good forecast is and show how a correct prediction is not necessarily the same thing as a good forecast. Most scenarios are going to be "wrong," but are never meant to be right. The test of this forecasting is not a more accurate picture of tomorrow, but better thinking about the future. The payoff is better decisions, not better predictions. If a forecast achieves this in an area of medium or high uncertainty, then it has succeeded.

> The test of this forecasting is not a more accurate picture of tomorrow, but better thinking about the future.

None of this implies that scenarios, or an "alternative futures" perspective, are the magic bullet, the "best" form of forecasting, always to be used instead of any other forecasting model. On the contrary, like quantitative forecasting, scenarios have their place. In the terms outlined in the previous chapter, they are appropriate for Level 2 and Level 3 uncertainty situations, where the world is complex enough and moving fast enough to outstrip the abilities of quantitative methods. It is senseless to make scenarios for low-uncertainty situations where extrapolative prediction methods are best or deeply uncertain situations where we can't make any meaningful judgments as to what is predetermined or isolate which assumptions we are unsure about.

Also, scenarios are only as good as the scenario process followed, and often it is followed poorly. The savvy forecast consumer should be on the lookout for scenarios that assign probabilities to scenarios—that is, create alternative views of the future only to say "this is the scenario we predict." The goal of scenario planning is not to predict, but to present and illuminate alternatives of how the external world will evolve to influence us. Scenario consumers should also beware of the many forms of low-grade scenarios, particularly heaven-and-hell scenarios (in one scenario, everything is completely perfect, and in the alternative scenario, everything is dramatically wrong), except where this is consciously done for future-influencing purposes. It is overwhelmingly likely that any future world will be a mix of good and bad, so all-good versus all-bad scenarios fail the plausibility test and offer no benefit as model future worlds in which to consider important decisions.

Notes

1. P. Wack, "Scenarios: Uncharted Waters Ahead." *Harvard Business Review* (September-October 1985), 73–89; and "Scenarios: Shooting the Rapids." *Harvard Business Review* (November-December 1985), 139–150.
2. With hindsight, it appears that a supply shock was very predictable, even probable. The warning signs were all there. Yet, by all accounts, Shell was the only one of the oil companies to have considered it and created contingency plans for it. The others were operating within a paradigm where oil was stable (at around $2 a barrel) as it had been for years.
3. Scenarios are sometimes constructed using a "backcasting" technique by which scenario builders consider a particular

prethought outcome that is worrying them—or that is anticipated by outside sources such as industry analysts or the media—and then trace its evolution back to the present through questions, such as, How could things change from now to lead us to that state of affairs? What events and responses could lead us to this future state?

4. A. De Geus, *The Living Company* (Boston: HBS Press, 1997).
5. Pierre Wack, quoted in A. Kleiner, *The Age of Heretics: Heroes, Outlaws, and the Forerunners of Corporate Change* (New York: Doubleday, 1996).
6. Cited at www.stevedenning.com
7. K. van der Heijden, *Scenarios: The Art of Strategic Conversation* (Chichester, UK: John Wiley & Sons, 2005).
8. "The Mont Fleur Scenarios," *Deeper News*, 7(1).

CHAPTER 10

Applying Forecast Filtering

THIS CHAPTER SEEKS TO ILLUSTRATE THE PROcesses of forecast filtering by applying it to sample forecasts that decision makers in business and policy areas might interact with in negotiating the future. The aim is to demonstrate how examples of real-world foresight may be probed following the principles developed in previous chapters.

The caveats in doing this are many. Most forecasts come in the form of documents and appendices running to hundreds of pages, which are of course too cumbersome to reproduce here. Necessity dictates that forecast extracts or executive summaries or media reports are used, with associated compromises. Obviously, forecast assessment itself may also be done at any length. The aim here is just to sketch the direction in which such analyses may proceed.

The forecasts below are chosen as more or less random samples, representative of their type. There is no intention to single out any organization or media outlet, and no implication that any source mentioned does better or worse forecasting work. In fact, each of the forecasts here merits serious attention, which cannot be said of all forecasts. The aim is not to point out the shortcomings of any particular forecast, but to identify the problems of approach that lead to good or bad future thinking. The source material tackled here is necessarily limited to forecasts that are in the public domain, publicly available, and not protected by purchase, so that the reader may be able to find and verify the original material. Most forecasts relevant to commerce are either company confidential or for sale.

The analyses presented aim to reproduce the conditions of reading the forecast "as is," that is, considering what is presented without assuming recourse to background information or investigation, in order to as closely as possible approximate a forecast consumer's experience of reading a forecast. Care has been taken to assess forecasts that still have a significant time to run (at time of writing, April 2008) because the challenge in forecast filtering is to be able to identify a forecast's merits without the 20/20 vision of hindsight. The current online location of each forecast has been provided. Copies are also available at www.futuresavvy.net.

AMERICA'S HOME FORECAST: THE NEXT DECADE FOR HOUSING AND MORTGAGE FINANCE

(2004-2013) [executive summary - extract]
Homeownership Alliance: www.homeownership.com
Report available at www.freddiemac.com/news/pdf/ americas_home_forecast.pdf

This study takes a long-term focus, producing ranges of forecasts for the next ten years (2004-2013) abstracting from potential cyclical fluctuations during this period. The study addresses the following topics: the outlook for housing demand and supply, including the impacts of net immigration on demographic trends; anticipated trends in the U.S. homeownership rate, considering prospective changes in the positions of major racial/ethnic groups in the population as well as prospective changes in homeownership rates for those groups; the outlook for home prices, focusing heavily on forecasts of per capita income growth as well as constraints on the supply of new housing; and the future of mortgage market demand and supply, with a discussion of factors that influence overall leverage.

The following remarks summarize the key findings of the study, and the Executive Summary concludes with brief consideration of some challenges and opportunities that lie ahead in the realm of public policy and potential public-private partnerships to address some of America's housing needs.

Summary of Key Findings

Housing Demand and Supply: Robust demand will require production of about two million new housing units per year, slanted heavily toward homeownership.

Demographic factors such as the size and age structure of the population will generate average household formations of 1.32 to 1.63 million per year during the next decade. This range is based on alternative projections of net immigration.

Household growth along with replacement requirements, second home demand, and changes in vacancies will require average production of 1.85 to 2.17 million new housing units per year. Even the lower end of this range is above the production levels of recent decades.

Conventionally built single-family homes will account for about 72 percent of total new housing units, an even larger share than during the past decade. Production of housing units in multi-family structures will account for nearly one-fifth of the total, and manufactured homes (HUD-code units) will account for the remaining one-tenth of the market.

The dollar volume of housing production, including new housing units as well as improvements to the stock of housing and commissions on home sales, will grow about in tandem with the overall economy. Housing's direct contribution to GDP—housing production plus services produced by the housing stock—should continue to account for about one-sixth of total economic output.

Homeownership: The national homeownership rate will rise above today's record level and most likely will exceed 70 percent by 2013.

Although the national homeownership rate has surpassed 68 percent, there are sizable differences in ownership rates across income levels, among racial and ethnic group,s and among different regions of the country.

A large number of factors affect the homeownership rate. Among the most significant drivers over the next decade will be the movement of recent immigrants into homeownership and continued growth in the number of baby boomers moving into their peak home-owning years.

A careful analysis of these trends suggests that the homeownership rate will increase over the next decade. The size of the increase will be affected by several factors including gains by racial and ethnic groups with historically low homeownership rates and the extent to which aging baby boomers choose to remain in their homes.

A rising homeownership rate will translate into at least 10 million additional homeowners by 2013 with roughly one-half of the gain accruing to minority households.

Home Prices: Home price appreciation should average around 5 percent per year from 2004-2013, but could be above 6 percent if supply constraints continue to tighten.

Home price gains have been unusually strong in recent years, because a combination of robust housing demand and increasingly stringent supply constraints in some areas (in turn caused by community concern about sprawl as well as shortages of developable land) has boosted price appreciation above the rate of income growth.

Home price growth that is in line with income growth is sustainable over the long run, even if home price appreciation outpaces overall inflation. A stable relationship between income and house prices over time argues against any nationwide "housing bubble." With the national unemployment rate below 6 percent (and falling), extremely low mortgage rates and economic growth accelerating, the likelihood of a decline in home prices at the national level is quite remote. Even at a local level, demand-supply conditions today are such that there are few, if any, markets that exhibit bubble characteristics.

Given the forecast of robust demand boosted by favorable demographics, continued tight supply conditions and no inventory overhangs, strong annual home price appreciation of around 5 percent is likely—although it could reasonably be as low as 4 percent or as high as 6 percent (especially if supply constraints continue). Additional increases in land use restrictions and regulation reducing developable land could boost home price gains still more, however, raising them above 6 percent per year.

Mortgage Demand and Supply: Mortgage originations are projected to average nearly $3 trillion per year and residential mortgage debt is projected to grow close to an 8.25 percent annualized rate.

America's families will likely need 125 million mortgage loans for home purchase or refinance, totaling $27 trillion in mortgage originations. First-time homebuyers will remain a major component of the purchase market, buying about 24 million homes over the next decade.

Residential mortgage debt outstanding is projected to grow by 8.25 percent per year, which would lead to more than a doubling of debt outstanding over the next 10 years, to $17 trillion.

Faster home price growth, related to land-use controls and other supply constraints, would translate into higher levels of originations and stronger debt growth. To illustrate, home price growth that is one percentage point faster than the projected base case would likely increase 10-year single-family originations to $30 trillion and increase residential mortgage debt outstanding to $19 trillion by the end of 2013.

The funds to support mortgage originations will primarily come from the sale and securitization of loans in the secondary market.

Access to global capital markets will continue to play an important role in financing mortgages for America's families.

✧ ✧ ✧

Analysis

This forecast was produced by the Homeownership Alliance, an advocacy organization that promotes individual home ownership in the United States. Its aim is to influence the issue of homeownership toward a future where more people are homeowners (with attendant economic and social benefits) and to broaden the base of homeownership in communities where this is not easily achievable. Although the alliance is clearly associated with advocacy, this is also the kind of baseline study that housing officials, industry analysts, and even property developers would consult.

The forecast—created in 2004—presents what appears to be a reliable if upbeat view of the coming decade. By 2013 they see the national homeownership rate exceeding 70 percent, which would mean about 10 million additional homeowners. They forecast home price appreciation averaging around 5 percent per year and say: "With the national unemployment rate below 6 percent (and falling), extremely low mortgage rates, and economic growth accelerating, the likelihood of a decline in home prices at the national level is quite remote."

In actuality, the housing bubble in the United States was over by the middle of the decade, and falling prices created foreclosures— the so-called sub-prime mortgage crisis—that have put extreme stress on mortgage lenders and the global financial system as a whole. The forecasts made are wrong. A key assumption on which the forecast was based–continued availability of cheap mortgages– changed, changing the future entirely.

There is a simple reinforcing feedback loop (see Chapter 8) at work, which is typical of all speculative bubbles. As house prices rise, the funding environment eases, which allows more borrowing, which allows new buyers to enter the market (or existing buyers to move up or speculate), which raises house prices. If one variable moves in the opposite direction—a housing price fall—then the same feedback loop will reinforce the driving down of house prices. Falling prices—that is, a falling asset base—will contract the funding environment (due to foreclosures and a falling asset base), which will squeeze buyers out, which will cause house prices to fall.

The forecasters do not miss the cheap mortgage assumption. They say, "The dramatic strength of the housing sector in recent years clearly was fueled by historically low interest rates. . . ." Their problem is they expected it to continue, or at least did not probe whether it would, or the conditions that would cause this key enabler of homeownership to disappear.

As we have seen in previous chapters, in any situation where there is reason to think the structuring conditions of tomorrow may be different from today, extrapolating trends is not going to give us a reliable forecast. In this forecast, the authors have extrapolated the various favorable trends that were active at that time, without looking to see if the forces behind them would continue to exist. The forecasters were also caught up in the bubble zeitgeist: In the era of easy money and rising prices, it is hard to see anything else.

Nobody could have predicted it one way or the other, of course. But there were certainly enough straws in the wind to be questioning the upward market assumption or the cheap money that came with it. If house prices increase rapidly, it is perfectly reasonable to expect them to come down (the pendulum effect). Elsewhere in the forecast, the report states then-current homeownership was at record levels (68.6% in the fourth quarter of 2003) and interest rates at historic lows, which suggests at least the possibility, if not the likelihood, of being in housing bubble territory. There was also evidence, for any forecaster willing to look, that large mortgages were being offered to non-prime borrowers and being repackaged and sold between financial institutions.

In other words, events as they have emerged were not or should not have been a complete surprise, and there was certainly a case for a scenario that explored contracting access to money and a housing price correction. Without predicting the future, a forecaster could have said: Either the present trends continue, based on positive economic and demographic trends and lagging supply, or alternatively, there is a contraction with downward-cascading effects for the housing market and homeownership. But, of course, a growing homeowner trend was exactly what the Homeownership Alliance wanted to see, and it was therefore unlikely to pour cold water on the picture with a contrarian view. In projecting then-current trends to continue they were, effectively, willing continuation of the good news into the future. This approach did not adequately prepare the forecast consumer for the reasonable spread of alternative outcomes.

WEST VIRGINIA CORRECTIONAL POPULATION FORECAST: 2005-2015 [EXTRACT]

State of West Virginia
Department of Military Affairs & Public Safety
Division of Criminal Justice Services
Criminal Justice Statistical Analysis Center, December 2006
Report available at http://www.wvdcjs.com/statsanalysis/publications/2005-2015_Forecast_Report_Final.pdf

This report describes the current correctional population in West Virginia (WV) and provides policymakers with a 10-year population forecast. Data is presented that indicates that WV's current correctional population has grown in recent years and will continue to grow over the next decade.

Correction Population Forecast

This section of the report presents the current 2005-2015 correctional population forecast, along with selected characteristics of this population. A backcast of the 2005-2015 forecast is also discussed. The backcast provides a means for evaluating the accuracy of the current forecast for the 2005 calendar year.

Previous forecast projections have been rather accurate. However, the potential for greater error increases with time. According to the 2004-2014 forecast report, for any given month since January 2001 forecast estimates have been within ±3.4% of actual population counts. The most recent correctional forecast update documented percent differences that fell within ±1.6% between the actual and forecasted populations (see Lester and Haas, 2006). Therefore, given the small amount of error associated with previous forecast projections, the current population projections can be anticipated to fall within this ±3.4% of the actual population over the course of the next year. This section begins with a presentation of the current forecast projections.

Current Forecast Projections 2005–2015

The results of the 2005-2015 forecast are presented in Graph 5. The forecast projections depicted in this graph represent all offenders in DOC custody, which includes Anthony Correctional Center (ACC), diagnostic, and local/regional jail inmates.

The actual correctional population is comprised of 5,312 inmates at the end of 2005. According to the current forecast, the correctional population is expected to grow at an average annual growth rate of 3.3% over the next decade. This will result in a correctional population that is expected to reach 6,192 inmates by the end of 2010 and 7,369 inmates by the end of 2015. This growth translates into a 38.7% increase in the total number of inmates confined in WV's adult correctional population between 2005 and 2015.

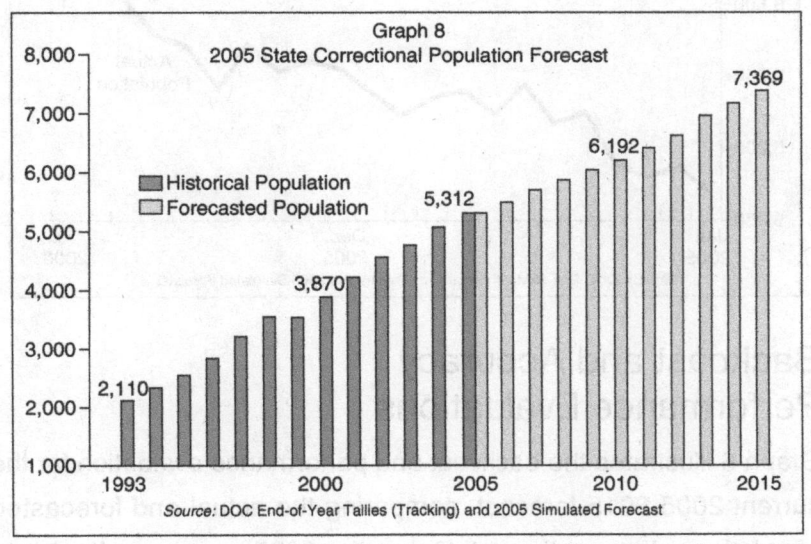

Graph 8
2005 State Correctional Population Forecast
Source: DOC End-of-Year Tallies (Tracking) and 2005 Simulated Forecast

Based on the average annual growth rate of 3.3% over the next ten years, DOC can expect to receive an average of 205 additional inmates per year. Once the known error that has been found to exist with previous forecasts has been considered, it is likely that the average will fall somewhere between 198 and 212 additional inmates over the next few years.

The projected growth in the correctional population over the next decade, however, is less than what the state experienced in the previous decade. Between 1995 and 2005, the state's correctional population increased at an average rate of 7.8% or 280 additional inmates annually. The result was a correctional population that more than doubled in the course of a decade. There was an 111.0% increase in the number of inmates in DOC custody, from 2,517 in 1995 to 5,312 in 2005. This is compared to a forecasted average annual growth rate of 3.3%, with a total increase of 38.7% between 2005 and 2015.

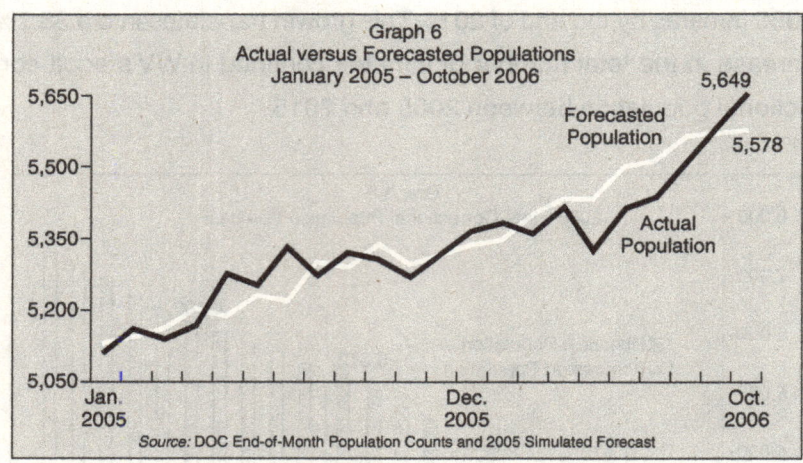

Backcast and Accuracy Performance Evaluations

Graph 6 illustrates the backcast and performance evaluation for the current 2005-2015 forecast, comparing the actual and forecasted populations. January through December 2005 represents the backcast period (one full calendar year prior to when the current forecast officially begins). As shown in Graph 6, the forecasted population closely paralleled the actual population over the course of the backcast period. The difference between the actual and forecasted population averaged 6 more inmates than the forecast model anticipated. This corresponded to an average difference of 0.1% over the backcast period.

Over the course of the 12-month period in 2005, population projections fell within plus or minus 2.1%. Percentage differences ranged from a high of 2.1% in July of 2005 to a low of 0.0% in December of 2005 (see Graph 6).

The performance accuracy of the current 2005-2015 forecast can be evaluated from January through October 2006. During this 10-month period, the difference between the forecasted and actual population of inmates averaged 26 more than actually existed. This corresponded to an absolute average difference of 0.5% over this time period.

Throughout this 10-month evaluation period, forecast projections remained fairly accurate with projections falling within plus or minus 2.2% of the actual population. Percentage differences ranged from a high of 2.2% in May of 2006 to a low of 0.3% in September of 2006 (see Graph 6).

Technical Description of the Model

The forecast of the state correctional population was completed using Wizard 2000 projection software. This computerized simulation model mimics the flow of offenders through the state's correctional system over a ten-year forecast horizon and produces monthly projections of key inmate groups.

The Wizard 2000 simulation model utilizes a technique that is consistent with that of a stochastic entity simulation model. It is stochastic, or probabilistic, in the sense that random numbers are used in the modeling process, and an entity simulation in the sense that the model is conceptually designed around the movement of individuals through the correctional system. The model is also generally an example of a Monte Carlo simulation technique, again because random numbers are used in the process of simulating the system. Individual cases (offenders admitted to supervision in WV) are processed by the model through a series of possible statuses (e.g., awaiting trial, prison, parole, and parole violation) based upon the transition probabilities fed in by the researcher.

Once the simulation model has moved the case to its new status, the process is repeated over and over until the case either reaches the end of the projection period, or enters what is referred to as a terminal. Terminal status signifies a complete exit from the system being modeled.

When a model is loaded with accurate data, it will prove to be quite reliable in forecasting a population, as it will mimic the actual flow of cases through the correctional system being modeled. The model operates under the notion of a "growing admissions assumption." This assumes, as stated in the introduction, that what happened last year will carry over to the next year. In order for the simulation model to work to its full potential, information must be gathered describing all of the entries and exits from the actual system for a previous one-year period. This applies to all offenders sentenced to the DOC custody. Additional data must be gathered describing the characteristics of the admission, confined, and release populations, parole hearings outcomes, and parole revocations. This information is then entered into the simulation model.

The Wizard 2000 simulation model for West Virginia was used to generate a ten-year prison population forecast. After several preliminary models, one model was produced to model the population accurately. The resulting model forecasts the state sentenced offender population according to their most serious offense. Anthony Correctional Center (ACC) and diagnostic inmates are entered separately into the model. The model is unable to provide forecast projections on specific characteristics of the ACC and diagnostic populations, due to their small sample size. This can be considered a limitation of the model.

The model requires the formation of offense categories, also referred to as ID groups. It is assumed that offenders within in each of the identified ID groups are handled by the criminal justice system in a similar fashion. In particular, it is assumed that offenders within each offense category are treated similarly in terms of factors related to sentencing, time served, and release decisions. Thus, specific offense categories or ID groups form the basis for all of the analysis contained in this report including the population forecast. These offense categories are murder, sex crimes, robbery, assault, burglary, property, drug, DUI, and "other" offenses. Each offender's most serious offense was used to construct the ID groups. In addition to the construction of ID groups, sentencing information is vital to the simulation model. There are a variety of descriptive statistics (minimums, maximums, and means) required from the sentencing data. These sentence calculations are described later in this section.

Forecast Assumptions

The Wizard 2000 simulation model simulates the movements of inmates through the prison system based on known and assumed factors affecting both the volume of admissions into the system and the lengths of stay for inmates who are housed in prison. It simulates the movements of individual cases, by offense category, and projects each separately.

The forecast model assumes that various factors known to impact trends in admissions and releases of inmates will remain relatively stable over time. It is assumed, for instance, that the sentencing composition for new commitments will remain the same as in the 2003 admissions. In addition, forecast projections assume the decision rates, which result in the granting of parole, will remain somewhat constant. The accuracy of the correctional population projections are contingent upon these assumption holding true over the forecast period.

❖ ❖ ❖

Analysis

In this forecast, the Criminal Justice Service for West Virginia is trying to figure out its future prison population levels. Its purpose is future-aligning: anticipating prison populations so that the prison service can prepare adequately to handle those numbers, in terms of buildings, facilities, staff, outside services, etc. (although the 37.8% increase forecast for 2015 may form part of a broader lobby for expanded facilities or a greater share of the state budget). Generally, however, the analysis is sober, technical, and not obviously operating in a bias-prone situation, nor taking any form of principled or ideological stance on incarceration, and we have no reason to think that the forecast is not the forecasters' best anticipation of the evolving situation. If one were providing services to the West Virginia Correctional Services, this would be the future view one would use.

The forecast has merits of certainty and clarity and arrives at specific forecast outcomes—an average annual growth rate of 3.3%

over the next decade resulting in a correctional population reaching 6,192 inmates by the end of 2010 and 7,369 by the end of 2015—that can be directly used in planning. However the forecast is not clear what will drive the growth trend, particularly in that the 1995-2005 growth rate was 7.8% (Graph 5). Without fully identifying the forces of change, the predicted fall from 7.8% to 3.3% growth is not adequately explained.

The forecasting method, which is specified and shared in some detail, uses a computerized simulation and projection software. As the authors describe it, the projections are an example of a "Monte Carlo" simulation technique, where random numbers are used to simulate possible criminal justice statuses—e.g., "awaiting trial," "prison," "parole," and "parole violation"—to mimic the actual flow of cases through the correctional system. (Transition probabilities are fed in by the researchers.) The forecasters' test of their model is to see whether it has been good for the period where both model data and real data is available, that is from January 2005 to October 2006, and refer to this verification process as "backcasting." In October 2006, as shown in Graph 6, the forecasted population closely parallels the actual population over the previous 22 months. The forecasters say: "The performance accuracy of the current 2005-2015 forecast can be evaluated from January through October 2006."

But is this an adequate check? Can we say that because a model proved accurate over a not-quite two-year period that it will be hold for a ten-year forecast? As we know, assumptions about the world are likely to hold in the short term, but not in the long term. So it is no surprise that the technical model proves adequate over two years. This tells us nothing about how it will hold up over ten years. If any key assumptions do change during this period, it will most certainly not hold up. The authors assert that "various factors known to impact trends in admissions and releases of inmates will remain relatively stable over time." But is it valid to assert this? How stable is the situation and how much change is likely?

In fact, the U.S. criminal justice system is subject to many social and political pressures and has often seen periods of high change, most notably in recent decades with tougher sentencing policies, particularly for first-time drug offenders, and ongoing privatization of the prison system. Although changes in sentencing appear unlikely in the forecast period, there is increasing vigilance and intolerance of some crimes types, for example sex crimes (including statutory changes pertaining to sex offenders including abolishing or restricting parole), which is likely to be a new driver of prison occupancy.

More generally, the current tough sentencing and parole environment has resulted in an all-time-high percentage of the U.S. population behind bars. This is a social and political issue, particularly because occupancy rates do not reflect the racial mix of the population as a whole—a powder keg that could go off at any time, creating profound pressures and possibly extensive changes. At the same time, questions keep being asked about the tax burden of unprecedented prison occupancy. Criminal justice has hardly proved immune from cost considerations in the past, and cost drivers may well change the future of criminal justice. Rising costs raise the attractiveness of alternative punishments, including community service orders. Technology also enters the picture, particularly as the ability to monitor offenders on parole has become more reliable and sophisticated. This suggests that new forms of parole and blends of inside/outside prison terms may become technologically feasible, and cheap, and may be used to drive down socially and financially expensive prison time.

It is, of course, uncertain how this will play out, but a good forecast would consider these factors, the uncertainties they cause, and how the uncertainties may resolve in different ways. There are certainly enough powerful social and economic forces at work to suggest that the assumptions the forecasters' have built their computer model around may not hold.

1.7M 'WILL HAVE DEMENTIA BY 2051'

BBC: www.bbc.co.uk, February 27, 2007
Full report (summary) available at http://www.alzheimers.org.uk/site/scripts/download_info.php?fileID=1

More than 1.7 million people in the UK will have dementia by 2051, costing billions of pounds each year, experts have forecast. The grim projections are based on the most up-to-date evaluation of dementia.

Currently 700,000—or one person in every 88 in the UK—has dementia, incurring a yearly cost of £17bn.

The government welcomed the London School of Economics and Institute of Psychiatry research, and said dementia care was already a priority.

The total number of people with dementia in the UK will increase to 940,110 by 2021, they predict. By 2051 the figure will be 1,735,087—an increase of 154% from now—which will mean dementia will affect the lives of around one in three people either as a sufferer, or as a carer or relative. This is mainly because of the UK's ageing population.

One in 20 people over 65 and one in five people over 80 has a form of dementia. Around two-thirds of those affected have Alzheimer's disease. There is no cure for dementia, and those with the condition need increasing care as the disease progresses.

'Piecemeal'

The researchers' investigations reveal caring for one person with late-onset dementia costs an average of £25,472 per year. Currently, the bulk of this cost is met by people with dementia and their families. Two-thirds of these people live at home—either alone or with friends or relatives. They said there were "marked variations" in the levels of provision and spending across the UK, and that care and support is "delivered piecemeal and in an inefficient fashion."

Professor Martin Knapp, of the London School of Economics, one of the report's authors, said: "This research highlights the desperate need for dementia to be made a national priority. Current levels of services and support for people with dementia and carers are clearly inadequate.

"Dementia is one of the main causes of disability later in life ahead of cancer, cardiovascular disease and stroke, yet funding for dementia research is significantly lower than these other conditions.

"Even delaying the onset of dementia by five years would halve the number of related deaths, saving nearly 30,000 lives annually."

'Intolerable strain'

Neil Hunt, chief executive of the Alzheimer's Society, added: "With every second ticking by, dementia costs the UK £539. We can't afford to ignore the true cost of dementia to society as a whole.

"We must tackle this huge challenge head on."

"We need to invest in dementia services, research, support and training and use what money is being spent more effectively. Planning now will save lives and money in the future."

He added: "This new research shows that the government is failing to support people with dementia and their carers."

"Dementia will place an intolerable strain on our health and social care system unless the right services and support are in place."

Older people's tsar Professor Ian Philp, who is currently preparing new guidance for local health and social care bodies on early intervention and support for people with dementia, said: "This is a significant report that highlights the key issues around dementia and its economic impact."

Health Minister Ivan Lewis said: "We welcome this important report which raises important issues around the future needs of people with dementia and provides a comprehensive picture of the economic burden of dementia.

"We have made a strong commitment to improving services for people with Alzheimer's disease and other forms of dementia and dementia has already been identified as a key healthcare priority."

Two drug companies—Pfizer and Eisai—are currently seeking a judical review with the aim of over-turning a National Institute of Health and Clinical Excellence (NICE) decision not to recommend the use of three drugs for patients in the early stages of Alzheimer's disease. NICE ruled that donepezil, rivastigmine, and galantamine should only be used to treat Alzheimer's once it has progressed to its moderate stages.

◆ ◆ ◆

Analysis

This is a media report of a *London School of Economics* and *King's College, London, Institute of Psychiatry* study, done for the *Alzheimer's Society*, predicting the number of British dementia sufferers will rise significantly in forty-five years (2006-2051). Although the forecast benefits from the credibility of the venerable organizations that put it out, and is therefore unlikely to be biased in any simple sense, its aim is clearly to influence the future—to put dementia on the national agenda and seek resources for research, treatment, and care. Publicity of the study is a necessary part of this, and the report exists to be widely publicized—for example, in media coverage, such as this story by the BBC.

The media treatment may or may not adequately represent the original study, so recourse to the original study is obviously the best way forward. But for reasons of time or availability, this is not always possible, and the news summary is often, in effect, all that the forecast consumer reads. This leads to a tricky situation, not least because the demands of news media require at least some contraction and simplification, and the tendency to focus on sensational outcomes. For example, the media report says that caring for one person with late-onset dementia costs "an average of £25,472 per year," and "the bulk of this" is met by people with dementia and their families. (The study itself says that 36% of care is undertaken by family members and unpaid caretakers, and is clearer that the financial figure includes a valuation of unpaid care.[1]) Also, the reporter often has to "storify" the study with on-day comment, such that it may become unclear what is part of the forecast and what is not. The contention that, "With every second ticking by, dementia costs the UK £539," is not in the forecast study.

The media treatment does not give the forecast method (they seldom do) but we may deduce that the current 2 to 3% per annum growth trends in dementia has been extrapolated to 2051 based on expectation of population aging. (As it happens, the fuller publicly available "forecast summary" is itself laconic on the methodology used, but does mention that ten leading UK and European experts used an "Expert Delphi Consensus" method "to produce the best possible estimates using currently available research data."[2] The full version of the study is, presumably, more detailed.) Nevertheless, the aging trend is a very secure one, and twinning the forecast to this trend has the merits of solidity and specificity.

On this basis, the report sees the number of dementia sufferers being two-and-a-half times today's figure by 2051, with resulting medical, social, and financial burdens going up accordingly. But we may ask, "Why are we looking to 2051?" This seems a very long forecast period indeed—way beyond the planning horizon of any government, financial, or commercial enterprise involved. There is no explanation of the length of forecast period. We may ponder whether a long-term view is used to dramatize the growth of the problem sufficiently—to raise the "worry level" of the forecast—because, in fact, the number of dementia sufferers is going up quite slowly. The study anticipates a rise in dementia sufferers from 700,000 to 940,110 in the years 2006-2021, which is an increase of 34% over fifteen years, or just 2.2% a year. Only when extrapolated to 2051 does the increase (154%) start to sound like a problem sufficiently serious to warrant public attention and resources.

There are wider forces at work, and plenty of money at stake in the future of dementia treatment. There is also always a faceoff between the British Government's National Health Service and interest groups, including multinational drug companies, on how much money is spent on treatment and which treatments are funded. This forecast is, in part, a salvo is this ongoing struggle. Although is difficult to tell what is going on behind the scenes, and there is no indication that anything untoward is happening, the forecast clearly plays a role in urging the government to spend more on the problem. Obviously, the higher the headline-increase figure, the better it suits the purpose of attracting public attention and resources.

More problematically, peering forty-five years into the rapidly changing, high-uncertainty future of medicine is no simple matter.

Knowledge of brain function is in flux, expanding rapidly, but still in its infancy. In forty-five years, it is entirely possible that dementia will be thought of in quite different ways to today, and it may be related to physical or social or environmental factors that are not yet conceived of and subject to remedies that are unimaginable today. It is likely that dementia diagnosis and treatments will look altogether different in 2051, as part of very significant world-changing improvements in medical technologies that significantly raise disease detection and life expectancy, among other things. (Widespread, extended human longevity may, in fact, raise dementia levels to numbers far *greater* than those anticipated in the forecast. On the other hand, the same medical technologies that postpone death may be used to tackle brain function, and dementia onset may be delayed.)

Furthermore, forty-five years will not only bring new technologies and new drugs, but also new business models and modes of service and product distribution in the medical field. Also, choices about how society will allocate medical resources in general, let alone to the elderly, or the poor elderly, may be made differently. Legal and moral issues will also profoundly affect this field, not least in defining how and to what extent we can interact with and "manage" human brain function. All in all, so much is uncertain about the medical, technical, financial, social, and moral questions pertaining to the future of dementia, that it is patently unwise simply to march a 2 to 3% growth in dementia forward by forty-five years, based on today's medicine and today's cost structure. This topic, for 2051, completely exceeds the limits of trend extrapolation, and any other form of quantification, and even our best techniques of judgmental analysis. There is no mid-twenty-first century forecast of dementia, determined in 2007, that can be any better than a wild guess.

Therein the prediction of 1,735,087 dementia sufferers in 2051 should be considered unreliable in the extreme. In fact, it's unlikely that the forecasters themselves really believe that exact number, but projecting to the last single sufferer is handy because, to the uninitiated, it signals diligence and accuracy in a forecast.

ENGLAND TO HAVE 13M OBESE BY 2010 [EXTRACT]

bbc.co.uk, viewed August 25, 2006

More than 12m adults and one million children will be obese by 2010 if no action is taken, a report by the Department of Health is predicting.

The Health Survey for England also warns 19% of boys and 22% of girls aged 2 to 15 will be obese.

The figures would mean the government would fail to meet its target to halt the rise in childhood obesity.

The report also says having two obese parents means children have five times the risk of being obese themselves.

One in four children in households where both parents are obese is obese themselves, compared to one in 20 in households where both parents are a healthy weight.

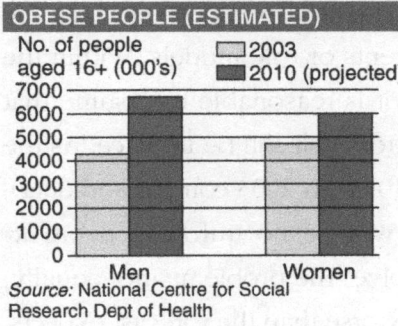

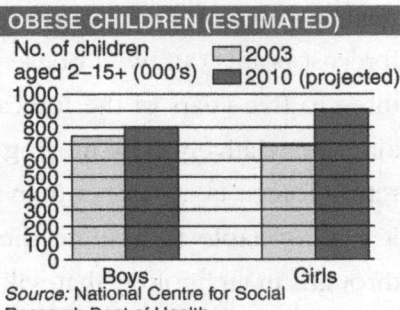

In households where one parent is obese, one in eight children is also dangerously overweight.

The report warns that, based on current trends, 33% of men and 28% of women will be obese by 2010.

The government says it is the "most accurate estimate so far" of future obesity rates.

The data is published just days after a "minister for fitness" was appointed.

◆ ◆ ◆

Analysis

In comparison to the previous UK study, this one is a perfectly reasonable topic and forecast time length for numerical trend extrapolation. It is valid to expect that the Department of Health has reliable data on obesity and, although the definition of obesity has changed a little over time (becoming stricter), the condition is not an area in rapid medical or societal transition between 2006 and 2010.

The trend to obesity is a dependable worldwide trend, driven by many consistent long-term factors. These are not mentioned in the media report, but are well known: easily available junk food, including at school cafeterias; sedentary lifestyles; and, in the UK, poor access to sport facilities in non-elite schools. Obesity also correlates with low socioeconomic status and prospects and, as the forecast points out, with obese parents or role models. Within the three to five years of the forecast, it is reasonable to assume that all these relatively slow-moving factors will still be in place. As the report forecasts no further than 2010 (with 2003 comparison data), it is reasonable to assume there will be no unforeseen breakthroughs in technology that will "solve" the problem, and, equally, no reason to see it get significantly worse than the forecast expects.

Clearly, the Department of Health's intention and mandate is to stop and reverse rises in obesity. Therein the forecast's intent is primarily future-influencing—to determine the size and scale of the problem and keep attention and resources focused on combating it. But the forecast is specific in saying that these forecast figures apply "if nothing is done." It is made clear to the reader that these numbers are, in effect, the "no action" scenario, but that this scenario is itself unreliable because the clear intention of government and allied interest groups is to make the future different from the forecast.

TOP FIRMS AND CLIENTS DELIVER VERDICT ON FUTURE OF LEGAL PROFESSION [EXTRACTS]

Lawfuel.com

http://www.lawfuel.com

Viewed February 19, 2008

- UNIQUE RESEARCH REVEALS LIKELY LEGAL LANDSCAPE in 2018
- Clients say rises in legal fees are unsustainable without more added value
- hegemony of magic circle dented
- expert legal advice will not be commoditized, BUT LAWYERS WILL NEED TO QUESTION WHAT IS CONSIDERED A 'PREMIUM' SERVICE
- legal services act UNLIKELY TO bring change at top of profession
- partners believe work-life balance and excellent client service is a 'contradiction in terms' [capitals in original]

The 'Law Firm of the 21st Century' study, carried out by leading legal researcher, RSG Consulting on behalf of Eversheds, outlines the views of 50 partners of 25 top law firms as well as general counsel, legal and financial directors at 50 of the world's most prominent companies. The report covers how the client/lawyer relationship is changing, the shape and structure of future law firms and trends in the way top clients are buying their legal services. In addition, it looks at what the impact of commoditization and standardization will be on top lawyers and clients, the perceived impact of the Legal Services Act and challenges associated with achieving a credible work-life balance.

The research also indicated a possible erosion of the dominance of Magic Circle firms, with a third of clients (34 percent), planning to buy legal services from firms outside the Magic Circle to get better value for money and better client service. Many felt there was little difference in the standard of legal advice between those firms inside or outside the Magic Circle.

Billing Trends

Rising fees and the cost of buying legal advice is the key concern among clients, with over half (55 percent) believing that the current growth in law firm fees was not sustainable. Controlling costs is a major concern for clients who are increasingly calling on their legal providers to justify fees and over half (53 percent) thought that lawyers needed to be more commercial and align themselves to their clients' business. But many top law firm partners are out of sync with their clients, with only 21 percent of them mentioning the need to control costs or add value as a concern.

The study highlighted the ambivalence lawyers and their clients have to the hourly rate. While most partners (82 percent) and clients

(86 percent) believe the hourly rate will be alive and well in ten years time, most acknowledged that it was not the most advantageous billing process for clients. A third of clients (32 percent), in turn, expressed their deep dislike for the billable hour.

Impact of the Legal Services Act and Trend Towards Commoditization

While the research revealed mixed views, the majority of partners (73 percent) did not believe the Act would result in significant changes to the partnership model and 72 percent of clients were similarly not very concerned about the impact of the Act. However, a significant minority of partners interviewed—20 percent—did expect to see major changes, including incorporation, and 42 percent of partners did foresee law firms taking outside investment, but it is likely be limited to mid-tier firms.

A significant minority of clients (24 percent) were concerned about whether a 'legal company' would be able to offer them same level of service, loyalty and commitment as a partnership.

When asked about the reported trends of a move towards commoditization of legal services, most partners and half of clients (53 percent) agreed that commoditization and standardization were significant trends in the legal market. However, they were not expected to eradicate the existence of the expert, individual lawyer as some commentators have predicted. 70 percent of partners believed that the type of work they did would be immune to commoditization and they actively wanted to avoid that trend in their practices. However, just over half the clients could see that commoditization was a potential way for private practice lawyers to add value.

◆ ◆ ◆

Analysis

This is a summary of a forecast of the future of the legal profession based on the opinions of lawyers and their clients (50 of each) who have been asked to look at the evolution of the industry. Although not much is said about the method behind the research, it appears that a questionnaire has been used, with simple collation of results (although a more complex questioning form such as Delphi Analysis may have been applied). Although respondent surveys inevitably frame perception due to the type of questions asked or not asked, and manner in which they are framed, there is no reason to suspect this one would not have been done as fairly as practically possible. Generally, insights into the future are all the better for being based on real fieldwork.

The problem is in who has been consulted. The forecasters have interviewed only senior lawyers (partners in top firms) and their clients. These are all experts in the industry, insiders to the field. On the one hand, insiders will have a finger on the pulse, and senior figures will have seen enough of life not to be swayed by alarmism or short-term trends. But insiders carry historical mental models of the industry and embody its business-as-usual assumptions and preconceptions, as well as its preferences. They are often the last to see how things could be done differently or to acknowledge or face up to the likelihood of change (which often directly threatens them).

One issue the research reveals is a disjuncture between law firms and clients over fees and value-for-money. On the one hand, this is to be expected—each side has different interests and will answer accordingly, even if only to signal to the other side. On the other hand, perception of poor value—low utility—does commonly point to a future resolution. It is clear that major clients are currently highly value-sensitive, and it won't take much to shift them into a partially or fully new way of managing their legal issues. In many industries, dissatisfied customers, once roused, turn not just to better-value competitors, but often to entirely new competitors with different approaches. Technology will play its part here. It is unlikely that an online distance service will ever substitute for subtle advice to prime clients facing complex legal issues, but routine procedures are, as the report suggests, prone to the commoditization and off-shoring that has been seen in many professions. In this part of the industry the cold winds of utility will drive the future, perhaps more than industry insiders are ready to see.

This is one example of how even interviewing a hundred insiders does not help this forecast escape industry "groupthink." Likewise, although many industry changing possibilities are perceived, they appear to have been more or less discounted by the survey respondents. It is likely that if more junior lawyers, or respondents completely outside the industry had been surveyed, a more rapidly and more profoundly evolving industry would have been seen and a more pressing sense of change would have resulted—better preparing law firms using this industry forecast to take these issues to heart and prepare for them.

USDA AGRICULTURAL PROJECTIONS TO 2017 [EXTRACT]
Interagency Agricultural Projections Committee, 2008
Report available at www.ers.usda.gov/publications/oce081/oce20081.pdf

Introduction

This report provides longrun projections for the agricultural sector through 2017. Major forces and uncertainties affecting future agricultural markets are discussed, such as prospects for long-term global economic growth and population trends. Projections cover production and consumption for agricultural commodities, global agricultural trade and U.S. exports, commodity prices, and aggregate indicators of the sector, such as farm income and food prices.

The projections are a conditional scenario with no shocks and are based on specific assumptions regarding the macroeconomy, agricultural and trade policies, the weather, and international developments. The report assumes that the Farm Security and Rural Investment Act of 2002 (the 2002 Farm Act), the Energy Policy Act of 2005, and the Agricultural Reconciliation Act of 2005 remain in effect through the projection period. Projections do not reflect the Energy Independence and Security Act of 2007. The projections are not intended to be a Departmental forecast of what the future will be, but instead are a description of what would be expected to happen under a continuation of current farm legislation, with very specific external circumstances. Thus, the projections provide a neutral backdrop, reference scenario that provides a point of departure for discussion of alternative farm sector outcomes that could result under different domestic or international assumptions.

The projections in this report were prepared in October through December 2007 and reflect a composite of model results and judgment-based analyses. Normal weather is assumed. Also, the projections assume no further outbreaks of plant or animal diseases. Short-term projections used as a starting point in this report are from the November 2007 World Agricultural Supply and Demand Estimates report.

✧ Long-Term Projections and the President's Budget Baseline

Projections in this report assume that biofuel blending tax credits and the 54-cent-per-gallon tariff on imported ethanol used as fuel are extended beyond their currently legislated expiration dates. This is in contrast to President's Budget baseline that assumes those tax credits and the tariff are not extended.

Overview of Assumptions and Results

Key assumptions underlying the projections include:

Economic Growth

World economic growth is projected to increase at a 3.5 percent average annual rate between 2008 and 2017, after averaging 2.9 percent annually in 2001-07. U.S. gross domestic product (GDP) increases from the 2007 slowdown toward a sustainable rate of about 3 percent over the longer term. Strong economic growth in developing countries, particularly important for growth in global food demand, is projected at 5.8 percent annually for 2008-17.

Population

Growth in global population is assumed to continue to slow to an average of about 1.1 percent per year over the projection period compared with an annual rate of 1.7 percent in the 1980s. Although slowing, population growth rates in most developing countries remain above those in the rest of the world. As a consequence, the share of world population accounted for by developing countries increases to nearly 84 percent by 2017, up from 79 percent in the 1980s.

The Value of the U.S. Dollar

The U.S. dollar continues to depreciate through 2011, with a drop in value of about 14 percent from 2002. Over the rest of the projection period, the dollar is assumed to show a small appreciation. Strong economic growth in the United States relative to the European Union (EU) and Japan will mitigate continuing pressure for the euro to appreciate relative to the dollar and will offset much of the trade-driven appreciation of the yen. In addition, capital continues to move into the United States to benefit from well-functioning and diverse financial markets.

Oil Prices

Large increases in oil prices over the past several years reflected strong demand for crude oil resulting from world economic recovery and rapid manufacturing growth in China and India. Following a continuation of increases through 2009, crude oil prices are expected to drop modestly in 2010 through 2013 as new crude supplies help offset the rise in demand from Asia. After 2013, oil prices are projected to rise slightly faster than the general inflation rate.

Underlying these longer term price increases, world oil demand is expected to rise due to strong global economic growth, particularly in highly energy-dependent economies in Asia. Factors expected to constrain longer run oil price increases include new oil discoveries, new technologies for finding and extracting oil, the ability to switch to non-oil energy sources, the ability to increase energy efficiency by substituting nonenergy inputs for energy, and continued expansion and improvement in renewable energy.

U.S. Agricultural Policy

The 2002 Farm Act, as amended, and the Agricultural Reconciliation Act of 2005 are assumed to continue through the projection period.

Area enrolled in the Conservation Reserve Program (CRP) is assumed to decline through 2009 as high prices encourage the return of some land to production when CRP contracts expire. CRP acreage is then assumed to gradually rise toward its legislated maximum of 39.2 million acres, reaching 37 million acres by the end of the projections.

U.S. Biofuels

The projections in this report were completed prior to enactment of the Energy Independence and Security Act of 2007. Thus, provisions of that legislation are not reflected in these projections, which are based on the Energy Policy Act of 2005.

The projections also assume that the tax credits available to blenders of biofuels (ethanol and biodiesel) and the 54-cent-per-gallon tariff on imported ethanol used as fuel remain in effect. Combined with the Energy Policy Act of 2005, State programs, high oil prices, and other factors, returns for ethanol production provide economic incentives for a continued expansion in the production capacity of the ethanol industry over the next several years. As a result, over 12 billion gallons of ethanol are assumed to be produced by 2010. Although more moderate growth is projected in subsequent years, over 14 billion gallons of ethanol are produced annually by the end of the projection period. Corn starch is expected to remain the primary feedstock for ethanol projection during the projection period. Cellulosic-based production of renewable fuels is assumed to meet the minimum specified in the Energy Policy Act of 2005 of 250 million gallons in 2013 and subsequent years. Biodiesel production is assumed to increase to near 600 million gallons by 2013.

Cattle and Beef Trade

The projections assume a gradual rebuilding of U.S. beef exports to Japan and South Korea. Due to recent changes in U.S. regulations, the projections assume Canadian cattle and beef from cattle over 30 months of age can be exported to the United States under the conditions that they are age-verifiable and born after March 1, 1999.

International Policy

Trade projections assume that countries comply with existing bilateral and multilateral agreements affecting agriculture and agricultural trade. The report incorporates effects of trade agreements and domestic policy reforms in place in November 2007.

Domestic agricultural and trade policies in individual foreign countries are assumed to continue to evolve along their current path, based on the consensus judgment of USDA's regional and commodity analysts. In particular, economic and trade reforms underway in many developing countries are assumed to continue.

The production of biofuels is experiencing rapid growth in a number of countries. The projections assume that the most significant increases in foreign biofuel production over the next decade will be in the EU, Brazil, Argentina, and Canada. In particular, the projections assume that the EU biofuel target of 5.75 percent of total transportation fuel use by 2010 is only partially met by that date, and is still not fully reached by 2017. Nonetheless, growth in biodiesel demand in the EU is a key factor underlying gains in global vegetable oils and oilseeds demand.

Key Results in the Projections

Steady domestic and international economic growth in the projection period supports gains in consumption, trade, and prices of agricultural products. Additionally, the projections reflect continued high crude oil prices and increased demand for biofuels, particularly in the United States and the EU.

U.S. Aggregate Indicators

- Although net farm income initially declines from high levels of 2007 and 2008, it is projected to remain historically strong throughout the projection period, and reach record levels beyond 2011. Growth in export demand contributes to increases in agricultural commodity prices and gains in farm cash receipts. Increases in corn-based ethanol production also provide a major impetus for this strong income projection. Higher commodity prices lower government payments for price-dependent program benefits, although annual CRP payments increase. With lower government payments, the agriculture sector relies increasingly on the market for its income. Cash receipts represent more than 90 percent of gross cash income in the projections, up from about 85 percent in 2005.

- The value of U.S. agricultural exports rises in the projections as steady global economic growth and stronger world trade lead to gains for U.S. agricultural export volumes and higher commodity prices. The lower value U.S. dollar is also an important factor underlying recent export gains and the projected growth. Additionally, higher commodity prices due to expansion of global biofuel demand contribute to the projected gains in export values. Increases in U.S. consumer income and demand for a large variety of foods underlie continued strong growth in U.S. agricultural imports.

- For most of the projection period, consumer food prices increase less than the general inflation rate. However, adjustments in retail prices due to higher energy and agricultural commodity prices lead to food price increases somewhat larger than general inflation in 2008 and 2009. Relatively large price increases are expected in 2008 for fats and oils and for cereals and bakery products, reflecting higher prices for vegetable oils and wheat. Consumer prices for red meats, poultry, and eggs exceed the general inflation rate in 2009 as the livestock sector adjusts to higher feed costs. Consumer expenditures for food away from home continue to grow in importance and account for more than half of overall food spending during most of the projection period.

U.S. Agricultural Commodities

- Strong expansion of corn-based ethanol production in the United States affects virtually every aspect of the field crops sector, ranging from domestic demand and exports to prices and the allocation of acreage among crops. A higher portion of overall plantings is allocated to corn. Higher feed costs also affect the livestock sector, mitigated somewhat by the increased availability of distillers' grains.
- Ethanol production in the United States continues its strong expansion through 2009/10, with slower growth in subsequent years. By the end of the projections, ethanol production exceeds 14 billion gallons per year, using almost 5 billion bushels of corn. The projected large increase in ethanol production reflects the Energy Policy Act of 2005, State programs, ongoing ethanol plant construction, and economic incentives provided by continued high oil prices. Feed use of corn declines in the initial years of the projections and then rises only moderately as increased

feeding of distillers grains helps meet livestock feed demand, particularly for beef cattle.

- Growth in the food use of wheat is projected to match the rate of population increase. Feed use of wheat rebounds from the low levels of 2006/07 and 2007/08 as higher corn prices encourage increases in wheat feeding. Wheat feeding then levels off as wheat prices relative to corn stabilize.

- Soybean acreage falls in the projections after 2008 due to more favorable returns to corn production. Longrun growth in domestic soybean crush is mostly driven by increasing demand for domestic soybean meal for livestock feed. Some gains in crush also reflect increasing domestic soybean oil demand for biodiesel production.

- Moderate expansion of domestic food use of rice is projected. Although growth is somewhat faster than population growth, it is well below the rates of growth in the 1980s and 1990s when per capita use rose rapidly. Imports of rice account for a growing share of domestic use in the projections.

- Mill use of upland cotton in the United States falls in the projections as U.S imports of apparel continue to increase, reducing domestic apparel production and lowering the apparel industry's demand for fabric and yarn produced in the United States.

- Duties and quantitative restraints on sugar and high fructose corn syrup (HFCS) trade between the United States and Mexico ended on January 1, 2008. This results in increased use of HFCS by Mexico's beverage industry and, consequently, larger sugar exports from Mexico to the United States.

- The production value of U.S. horticultural crops is projected to grow by more than 3 percent annually over the next decade, with consumption of horticultural products continuing to rise.

Imports play an important role in domestic supply during the winter and, increasingly, during other times of the year, providing U.S. consumers with a larger variety of horticultural products.

- Production of all meats slows or declines in the first half of the projections, largely reflecting higher feed costs and lower producer returns as more corn is used in the production of ethanol. After those production adjustments, strong domestic demand and some strengthening in meat exports result in higher prices and higher returns, providing economic incentives for expansion in the sector.

- Per capita meat consumption declines through 2012-14 as the livestock sector lowers overall production and retail prices rise. Meat conumption per person then rises again at the end of the projections period. Rising incomes facilitate gains in consumer spending on meat. Nonetheless, overall meat expenditures represent a declining proportion of disposable income.

- Strong domestic and international demand for dairy products contributed to high U.S dairy prices in 2007. Despite higher feed costs, strong farm-level milk prices are projected to encourage further increases in milk cow numbers through 2009. Combined with an upward trend in output per cow, the results are relatively strong gains in milk production in 2008 and 2009 and decreases in milk prices. Smaller production gains are projected on average over the rest of the projection period because milk cow numbers decline after 2009. Milk prices rise after 2009.

Agricultural Trade

- World consumption of many grain, oilseed, and meat commodities has exceeded world production in the past several years, reducing global stocks. As a result, global stocks-to-use ratios have dropped sharply and prices have risen. Tight market conditions are projected to persist for many commodities over most of the coming decade, keeping agricultural commodity prices high.

- Broad-based global economic growth provides a foundation for robust gains in world demand for agricultural products. Economic growth in developing countries is especially important because food consumption and feed use are particularly responsive to income growth in those countries, with movement away from staple foods and increased diversification of diets. Rapid expansion of ethanol and biodiesel production in some countries also adds to global agricultural demand growth.

- Population growth rates are slowing in most countries but rates in developing countries remain nearly double those of developed countries. Many developing countries are also projected to achieve rapid economic growth rates.

- The United States will remain competitive in global agricultural markets, although trade competition will continue to be strong. Expanding production in a number of countries, including Brazil, Argentina, Canada, Ukraine, and Russia, provides competition to U.S. exports for some agricultural commodities. The lower-valued U.S. dollar assumed in the first half of the projection period boosts U.S. agricultural competitiveness and export growth. Even as the U.S. dollar strengthens later in the projection period, export gains continue to contribute to gains in cash receipts for U.S. farms.

- Continuing growth in the livestock sectors of developing countries in Asia, Latin America, North Africa, and the Middle East accounts for most of the growth in world coarse grain imports projected during the next decade. The United States is the major corn exporter in the world. However, with increasing use of corn for U.S. ethanol production, U.S. corn exports show very little growth through 2012/13. In response, corn production and exports are assumed to increase for Argentina, Ukraine, Republic of South Africa, and Brazil. China is also assumed to increase corn production, which changes its net corn trade by slowing the decline in its exports and the increase in its imports. Nonetheless, China is projected to become a net importer of corn in the longer run, reflecting declining stocks of grain and increasing demand for feed for its growing livestock sector.

- Vegetable oil prices rise in response to rapidly increasing demand for food use in low- and middle-income countries. Vegetable oil prices also rise relative to prices for oilseeds and protein meals because of expanding biodiesel production in a number of countries. Brazil's rapidly increasing soybean area enables it to gain a larger share of world soybean and soybean meal exports, despite increasing domestic feed use. Argentina is the leading exporter of soybean meal and soybean oil, reflecting the country's large and growing crush capacity, its small domestic market for soybean products, and an export tax structure that favors exports of soybean products and biodiesel rather than soybeans. The former Soviet Union, Eastern Europe, and Southeast Asia increase rapeseed and palm oil production for use as biodiesel feedstocks.

- The United States, Australia, the EU, Canada, and Argentina have historically been the primary exporters of wheat, although exports from the Black Sea region have grown in the past 10 years. Over the next decade, Russia and Ukraine are projected to have a growing importance in world wheat trade, reflecting low costs of production and continued investments in their agricultural sectors. However, high year-to-year volatility in these countries' production and trade can be expected due to typical weather-related variation in yields.

- Cotton consumption and textile production are projected to increase in countries where labor and other costs are low, such as China, India, and Pakistan. China is the largest importer of cotton in the world. Although China's cotton imports are expected to grow more slowly than the rapid gains since 2001, these increases account for most of the gains in global cotton trade in the projections. The United States continues as the world's leading cotton exporter, reflecting its large production capacity and its reduced domestic mill use of cotton as apparel imports continue to grow.

- Long-grain varieties of rice account for around three-fourths of global rice trade and are expected to account for the bulk of trade growth over the next decade. Indonesia, the Philippines, and Bangladesh become the three largest rice-importing countries and account for about 30 percent of the increase in global rice trade over the next decade. Sub-Saharan Africa, a large importing region, accounts for more than a fourth of the increase in trade, with the Middle East also contributing to rice trade gains. Thailand, Vietnam, the United States, India, and Pakistan remain the world's largest rice-exporting countries.

- U.S. meat exports benefit from strong foreign economic growth. However, even with U.S. beef exports to Japan and South Korea assumed to gradually rebuild, total U.S. beef exports do not return to levels of 2000-03 until late in the projection period.

- Pacific Rim nations and Mexico are key markets for long-term growth of U.S. pork exports. Higher income countries of East Asia increase pork imports as their domestic hog sectors are constrained by environmental concerns. Mexican pork imports rise rapidly, driven by increases in income and population. Brazil is constrained in its pork trade by the presence of foot-and-mouth disease, but continues to be a major pork exporter to markets such as Russia, Argentina, and Asian markets other than Japan and South Korea.

✦ Brazil remains a leading poultry exporter as low production costs allow the Brazilian poultry sector to remain competitive in global trade. Poultry exports from countries affected by avian influenza, such as Thailand and China, are expected to be mostly fully cooked products destined for higher income markets.

✦ ✦ ✦

Analysis

This forecast summary—put out by the U.S. Department of Agriculture with a future-aligning purpose to broadly help businesses, policymakers, and various other stakeholders plan for the future in this area, is worth running at some length because it is close to a model approach in various respects. The USDA has a responsibility to be evenhanded and not indulge in bias and spin. This report is demonstrably evenhanded and nonideological, even though agriculture can be the subject of some of the most rabid policy and ideological debates of our era, including carbon neutrality, sustainability, GMOs, pesticide use, and other hot-button topics. International trade policy is equally a political football, and the tendency of forecasts in such areas is to argue an agenda, or politely say nothing of value, neither of which problem manifests in this work. The USDA is not even swayed by patriotism to be necessarily upbeat about U.S. interests.

The forecast is also remarkable for constructing its view based on clear identification of the forces that affect the future (drivers and blockers of change) and clear explication of the assumptions made about each one. It only moves into the future after determining what drives change in the field in the first place and making considered assumptions about how these drivers will play out in themselves (before considering how they will affect each other or the overall future of agriculture and agricultural trade). This means that better forces and assumptions have been built into the forecasting model. This also puts the reader in a good position to critically follow the process—agreeing or disagreeing on the setup—and considering the conclusions accordingly.

On this firm basis, the forecast determines expected outcomes using both judgmental and quantitative methods, which is reasonable for the time period forecast. It is rich and specific in elucidating outcomes that can be taken forward by planners. Moreover, it is clear about the pace of change and works fully over the forecast time period (saying for example, that oil prices will rise to 2009, fall back, then rise again after 2013.) Regardless of whether these assessments are correct, the attempt to think through the time period not merely to the end of it is valuable to decision makers planning for shorter horizons.

The authors are keenly aware that if factor assumptions change, the forecast will deteriorate. They are therefore specific in saying the forecast is what may be expected to occur under a continuation of current agricultural legislation and specific assumptions about external conditions. They have, in effect, in the parlance of foresight work, created a "baseline scenario" for the future of agriculture and agricultural trade. In this sense, the forecast remains a direct prediction and is therefore vulnerable to having made poor judgments about key drivers, enablers, or blockers, or the pace at which they emerge, or the effect they have on each other. The only way to escape this would be to explore different outcomes based on different assumptions about how the structuring factors could evolve, in effect creating alternative scenarios each with an alternative mix of factor inputs (for economic growth, the U.S. dollar, the oil price, biofuel emergence, trade policy, new technologies, and so on), which would lead to outcomes different from the one predicted. This would create more "stretch thinking" and a more robust view, particularly if the world changes fast in this area.

Notes

1. Alzheimer's Society, *Dementia UK, Summary of Key Findings* (London: Author, 2007), p. 9.
2. Ibid., p. 3.

CHAPTER 11

Questions to Ask of Any Forecast

FORECASTS ARE AN INDISPENSABLE BUT HIGHLY patchy guide to the world of tomorrow. We take them seriously because understanding future conditions and requirements is key to future success, but we need to assert strong independence of mind as to whether any forecast is valid. By asking tough questions to quickly and effectively evaluate forecasts, we can extract the value they possess, without being duped by bias, cowed by expert credentials, or bamboozled by fancy software.

The remainder of this chapter condenses the argument of the book as a whole, thematically grouping the test questions to ask of any forecast in one easy-reference list.

Purpose

What is the purpose of the forecast? What can be gleaned about why it exists, who put it out, or what the intention of the forecaster was? Is the forecast upfront about its purpose?

All forecasting is done for benefit. By recognizing the interests at work behind a forecast, assessing what benefit or benefits are sought by the forecaster or whoever commissioned the forecast, one can make a better judgment as to potential strengths and weaknesses. We may ask, What effect or concerns is the forecast trying to arouse? How is it legitimating a view that the forecaster or forecast organization holds, or actions it wants to take or prevent others from taking? What future change is sought or being legitimated?

Is the forecast future-aligning or future-influencing?

Forecast benefit falls into two main categories: future-aligning benefit where forecasters anticipate change in order to adapt early and successfully to it; or a future-influencing benefit, where forecasters are trying to influence the future. Future-aligning approaches aim to be objective in giving their best reading of a most likely outcome or outcomes. They may fail, but the intention is there, so, on balance, this approach will be more accurate. Future-influencing forecasts aim to succeed on other terms—alerting and shaping opinion, changing minds, and harnessing action.

Ideally, a forecast will be clear in distinguishing between a desirable (or ideal) outcome and a probable one, but this is made tricky because often forecasts contain both future-aligning and influencing aspects, and also because future-influencing forecasts are stronger if they appear neutral and are therefore often disguised as such. Nevertheless, a future-influencing intention can be identified by asking:

- **Is the forecast widely publicized?** If a forecast seeks publicity, it is very likely to have future-influencing intent. A future-aligning forecast is usually a competitive document, for the benefit of the forecasters or those who commissioned it, and is usually proprietary during the forecast period.

- **Does it specify action to take in the external world?** While future-aligning forecasts often contain action recommendations, these are mainly inwardly focused, advising how to act to promote organizational alignment with what is expected. In a future-influencing forecast, by contrast, the forecaster inevitably asks the reader to act in the external world, to sign up, speak up, or join up to help change the future.

- **Is it a forecast of extremes?** Future-influencing forecasts are often pictures of extreme optimistic or pessimistic outcomes—utopias to be aspired to or dystopias to be avoided—which are a motivation tool in getting people to join a future-influencing agenda. The future is very likely to contain a mix of good and bad, just like the present and the past.

Specificity

Is the forecast mode predictive—spelling out what will happen—or speculative, illuminating possible alternatives?

Although there is some overlap in practice, forecasts divide into those that are trying to accurately predict the future versus those that are trying to illuminate alternatives that may arise. The former offers the benefit of advising what will happen but it is highly likely to be wrong; the latter offers the benefit of capturing the spread of plausible or probable outcomes (sometimes written up as scenarios) but does not commit to a clear prediction.

Is there too much certainty?

Certainty is a warning sign. In short-term situations, or closed systems with few variables, the attempt to pinpoint outcomes is reasonable. But the forecast consumer should consider claims to medium- and long-term accuracy with acute skepticism. Predictive forecasts that go beyond contained low-uncertainty situations are almost certainly worthless.

Is there enough certainty? Is the forecast hedging?

While predictive certainty is a red flag, the opposite is also a weakness. Forecasters sometimes equivocate about what might happen behind hedged statements to the point where the forecast is so vague about outcomes and time frames that it is valueless.

Whether predictive or speculative, good forecasts are compelling in their detail. They take a stand and define what changes they see and how and why they will come about. They give the reader a concrete sense of how a new reality would look and feel and specify a full and reasoned path to the future. The speculative forecast may allow for a number of alternative outcomes, but will detail each one.

Is the forecast clear about the pace of change? Does it specify timelines or does it leave the question hazy?

It is one thing to show that the conditions for change exist. It is another, altogether more difficult task to be able to forecast the pace of change, that is, to provide the "when" in addition to the "what" for the prediction, or for alternative scenarios. Anticipated events detached from time period are not worth much.

In poor forecasts the reader is often left with fuzzy phrases about time such as: "We can expect that . . ." or: "In the future there will be . . ." A better forecast will specify not only how far into the future it looks, but specify a timeline or identify milestones along the way to a predicted outcome. Tackling the problem of timing forces forecasters to think very carefully through the drivers and blockers of change, and particularly to clarify their argument about why and how blockers will be overcome.

Information Quality
How extensive and how good is the base data?

Data is never as solid as it seems. The difficulties in getting numbers that are an accurate reflection of the world—which bedevils studies of the present as well as the future—are immense. Among these are problems in validity of definitions, validity of sampling, how research is skewed by the form of the research or particular questions asked, or by how resulting information is judged and collated.

Better forecasts provide data that has been or can be independently corroborated. They also explain the data research method where applicable, along with its strengths and weaknesses, and provide the full set of results rather than selectively dropping juicy numbers into the analysis.

Particular questions to ask of data in forecasts are:

- **Is the data up to date?** Forecasts sometimes use data from decades ago, assuming or pretending the picture of the world they present is still valid.
- **Does the forecast use secondary data?** It is very common that "big-picture" future views use data created by others, often bringing together facts and numbers from many sources into one study. This risks disconnection with context and statistical caveats that frame the primary research. Also, secondary

data goes through a laundering and "broken telephone" effect, and this is exacerbated when forecasts are reproduced in the popular media.

- **Is the data real or a projection?** Sometimes data given are not real recorded figures but "future" data points that have been projected from past data, which raises obvious questions about how this projection has been done and how valid the process is. A good forecast will carefully distinguish real data from projected data.

Interpretation and Bias
Are the forecast's biases natural or intentional?
There is no such thing as a perfectly neutral or objective view of the future. All forecasts contain the interpretations and biases of those who made them. We should expect this natural bias, and distinguish it from intentional bias, where forecasters are fixing the numbers or making other sins of commission or omission in misrepresenting likely outcomes.

The biased forecaster has many ways of selecting, placing, or spinning the facts. The key indicators of intentional bias are:

- Selective choice of facts, or omission of opposing or inconvenient data
- Prejudicial organization or emphasis
- Emotional words
- Letting worst case stand for the whole

What is the reputation of the forecaster and forecast organization? Does the forecaster have anything to lose by being wrong? Is there "skin in the game"?

Bias comes mainly from forecasters trying to influence the world, and often their dodgy reputation precedes them. A good reputation is no guarantee against bias, of course. But a forecaster or forecast organization with a good reputation has something to lose from a biased forecast. Generally, it is heartening if there is cost to the forecaster or forecast organization for being wrong, and this is all the stronger if there any evidence of real investment of any kind based on the back of the forecast. As ever, actions speak louder than words.

Are bias-prone contexts at hand?

The forecast filterer should be on the lookout for bias-prone contexts, asking:

- **Is the forecast sponsored?** Who paid for it and why? Why now? More generally, who brought it into being? What are their general intentions and what is their specific agenda here? Better forecasts will state the conditions behind their emergence.

- **Is self-interest prominent?** Anywhere where forecasters view the future in a way that obviously benefits themselves, bias is likely. The forecast consumer should ask how this benefit influences what is said. Here bias is not limited to forecasts with a macro-agenda to change the world. It may be a company or nonprofit organization that manipulates data or interpretation in its own interest, or a government agency deflecting or postponing difficult questions into the future through asserting a rosy forecast. Self-interest is also at work when the forecasting organization stands to benefit from funds allocated to address a future problem that it itself forecasts.

- **Are ideology and idealism prominent?** Where an ideology is behind the forecast, bias is not inevitable, but it is more likely. (When we, as forecast consumers happen to agree with the ideology espoused it is often harder to see that it is an ideological stand.) Forecasts that are more agnostic on policies and principles are on average more reliable.

- **Does the forecast focus on a "single issue" future?** Where a forecast prioritizes a single issue as dominating the future—bio-terror, renewable energy, or human aging, for example—chances are the forecaster is compromising the truth or reasonable analysis to propose this extreme view.

- **Is editorial oversight bypassed?** The editorial process provides peer review and judgment on forecast material and generally limits or verifies extreme views before they are pushed out into the world. Where editorial oversight is lacking, for example, in the many new self-publishing options on the Internet, the forecast may not have gone through any peer review.

Methods and Models

Does the forecast specify its methods?

A forecast takes us from present conditions to future outcomes: In every case there is a method for getting from the present to the future, even if that "method" is pure intuition. A good forecast will state its primary methods, including the limitation and biases thereof. The author will show his or her working, revealing a train of logic that one can follow and agree with, or not. Poor forecasters will be unaware of their primary method or unable or unwilling to state it.

This does not imply that highly methodological forecasts are better. Often formal methods give the illusion of process when it is not there. A forecast can be overloaded with method and short on basic insight and common sense.

Does the forecaster imply the method is too complex, too arcane, or too proprietary to share?

Forecasts that don't spell out their method sometimes offer excuses such as mathematical complexity or nondisclosure policies. Even where full accounting cannot be given, in every case enough should be said about forecast methods for the forecast consumer to be able to judge the process. If it sounds like an obscure or arcane methodology is at work, chances are the forecaster has not followed the process he or she wants consumers to think was followed, or entirely thumb-sucked the prediction.

The existence or claim of complex methods and fancy analysis is often in itself a warning sign of a bad forecast. The forecaster may be oblivious to or even obscuring the vulnerability of the model's key assumptions with color graphics and fancy math.

Do forecast proponents trumpet their unique, or "new and improved," methods?

Forecasts or their purveyors often claim forecast quality based on unique methods only they possess. While some forecasters will have better methods than others, there are no magic bullets in forecasting. Sometimes forecast purveyors attract attention, not to mention sales, by claiming a "new" forecasting method that is more accurate and more reliable than past methods. Users—who may have been disappointed in the past—are assured that this time they can absolutely depend on the predictions generated. This is a sales pitch, if not snake oil.

Quantitative Limits

Is the use of quantitative methods appropriate?

When presented with a forecast based on quantitative processes, the forecast consumer should ask, Is this a valid domain for quantitative analysis? Quantitative forecasting works well in low-uncertainty, relatively closed, short-term forecast situations, where it is reasonable to say that key assumptions will hold during the forecast period. For other forecasts it is inappropriate. No matter how pretty the math or how powerful the computer, one mistaken assumption will still send the analysis barreling down the wrong path.

Most forecasts of the future are, whether they know it or not, taking on high-uncertainty situations, where we cannot know which factors affect which others, when, at what rate, and by how much, or even if we have taken all the necessary factors into consideration. These forecasts address situations that are, in fact, "chaotic" or that can fairly be seen as "wicked problems." While quantitative methods may help forecasters think about them, they cannot safely predict the future under these conditions.

Is a machine doing the thinking?

Where quantitative and statistical methods are used, forecasters sometimes let computers do their thinking for them, producing results that don't pass even the most basic commonsense test. Much of forecasting is commonsense, asking simple fundamental questions about drivers and blockers, over and over again. A sensible, thinking person who asks the right questions can forecast as well as any fancy program that is merely finding elaborate answers to the wrong questions. Nothing is more sophisticated than commonsense.

Managing Complexity

Does the forecast oversimplify the world?

Most situations in the world have infinite variables and outcomes. Poor forecasters determine the simple progression of one issue while assuming the rest of the world stands still. Good forecasts distill this complexity and narrow the uncertainty, but don't oversimplify the irreducible future uncertainty of multifactorial situations. In complex situations, good forecasts make provision for alternative and unexpected outcomes.

Does the forecast acknowledge systemic feedback?

Systems dynamics provide some grip on complexity, showing how variables are linked in a cause and effect chain, with feedback loops, which helps avoid a simplistic cause-and-effect model of the world. A good forecast will investigate how the system works—what typically affects what, and in what order, with what feedback potential—to determine the net effects of a primary change, including or potential opposite effects or side effects. It will account for the power of systemic feedback to reinforce and accelerate a change, or balance and block it.

Does the forecast anticipate things that could speed up the future, or push it off track? Does it account for triggers and tipping points?

A good forecast will not assume a steady evolution from the present or a constant rate of change. It will see the effect of critical mass and be ready for reinforcing or balancing thresholds crossed, leading to rapid acceleration or deceleration of change or a sharp change the direction of an established trend.

Does the forecast expect exponential change?

Rapid change is all around us, but change is exponential only under very specific, unique circumstances, and never dependably so. It is safe to discount all predictions that assume exponential change, unless the forecast tells you the period for which exponential change is valid, and why this is expected. If exponential change were common, most forecasts would underestimate change. In fact, mostly change is grossly overestimated, particularly in the short term.

As simple systems dynamics shows us, there is a strong and ultimately overwhelming tendency of phenomena to move toward equilibrium and for change to be arrested or reversed. An understanding of S-curve or oscillating behavior reins in future thinking that assumes indefinite exponential effects.

Assumptions and Paradigm Paralysis

Every forecaster makes assumptions: Assumptions are the basis on which present conditions are turned into a view of the future. Forecast consumers should ask the following questions about a forecast's assumptions:

- **Has adequate horizon scanning been done?** A wide and thorough view of the forces and trends acting on a situation is an indicator that the forecaster has thought beyond his or her immediate frames. There's no guarantee of course, but a full scan of the outside world commonly throws up problems that may lead to questioning common assumptions.

- **Are the assumptions stated? Is the forecaster aware of his or her own assumptions? Is the forecaster willing to entertain alternative assumptions?** A better forecast will realize, acknowledge, and specify its assumptions about society, technology, human nature, legislative developments, etc., that underlie the forecast and argue for their pertinence. It will be clear about how its assumptions lead to its forecasts, and how other assumptions may lead to alternative outcomes. If no assumptions are identified, it is likely that the forecaster is assuming that existing trends will evolve at their current rate, which is a poor assumption.

- **Do the forecaster's assumptions appear valid and reasonable?** A forecast is only as good as its assumptions. If the assumptions fail, the forecast will fail, no matter what model or technique is used. Obviously, it is not possible to tell which assumptions are good or poor until the future actually plays out, but this does not prevent the savvy forecast consumer questioning the assumptions made and positing the effect of others that may have been missed.

Zeitgeist and Groupthink

Is the zeitgeist speaking through the forecaster?

A poor forecast will, consciously or unconsciously, assume that currently dominant perceptions, needs, wants, concerns, and aspirations will be still dominant in the future—it will be held hostage by the current zeitgeist. History shows that the issues framing the present and recent past will inexorably evaporate, to be replaced by others, and a good forecast will anticipate these shifts even if it can't see them.

Is the forecast jumping on the bandwagon?

Generally, it is better if many sources are saying the same thing or making the same forecast. Corroboration is reassuring and it is usually better not to put much stock in a lone voice. However, while consensus is good, it is not infallible, and consensus-based forecasts are particularly vulnerable to a bandwagon effect or "groupthink," where everyone predicts the same thing because everyone else is. A good forecast will not easily be sucked into the prevailing wisdom and will question general consensus before buying into it.

Does the forecast rely on "experts"?

Experts are necessary in a specialized world, and expertise and credentials are important in forecasting, but experts are wrong as much as anyone. A field's experts are particularly likely to be heavily invested in the status quo, and be expert precisely in its existing procedures, attitudes, and prejudices. Change often comes from outside and experts are often the last to see it.

Does the forecast do stretch thinking? Does it allow us to break free from "the official future"?

While we should question forecasts thoroughly, we should not automatically seek to tone down forecasts of unlikely outcomes, or filter out creative or fringe thinking where new possibilities or threats are anticipated. This is often the juice in the forecast, and all too often there is lamentably little of it. As we have seen, the tendency to overestimate and overimagine change is the more likely failing in forecasting. But forecasts also weaken themselves by being too timid or too conservative, particularly in exploring effects and implications of a primary innovation.

Sometimes the world does go in implausible directions, away from the "official future," and a forecast should take us there. A good forecast credibly stretches the mind. Once a genuine case for change has been made, a good forecast will fill out the details and look for all the possible resulting effects and explore possible ensuing capabilities and problems. As Isaac Asimov is reputed to have said, "the difficult thing to forecast is not the car, but the parking problem."

Drivers and Blockers

Whether future change occurs depends on the outcome of the ongoing power struggle between the forces in favor of change—drivers and enablers, on the one side, and friction and blockers on the other. We should ask:

Are change drivers and enablers identified? Or are trends simply projected?

Trends are evidence of underlying drivers of change at work. A poor forecast will take a trend at face value, assuming its continued evolution. A better forecast will determine what forces are driving the trend, and how durable or vulnerable these are, before assuming a constant, incremental evolution.

Drivers are assisted by enabling conditions, which may be such elements as friendly international relations, high investment in R&D, benign legislation, for example. A good forecast will identify necessary enabling resources necessary for change to go forward—what else must happen around the particular change forecast for that change to happen—and will show that these enablers will be in place.

Are blocking forces identified and fully accounted for? Is friction factored in?

All drivers of change work against the frictional resistance of the status quo—the systems and solutions that people are currently invested in and comfortable with. They also face direct blockers, which are forces that have a vested interest in the status quo and don't want to see change, or that have an interest in another type of change.

A good forecast will assess the strength of resistance to change and anticipate specifically if and how this resistance will be overcome, if indeed it will be, and account for the resources required to achieve this. Rather than running with the breathless wow-of-the-new, the forecast will display a measured pragmatism in the face of constraints, and adjust the forecast direction and/or timing accordingly.

When looking for key drivers and blockers, we should particularly ask:

- **Have utility questions been asked and adequately answered?** No matter how stunning an innovation or how unprecedented a technology, it will only emerge into the world at large if it favorably improves the cost-benefit equation (including the cost of overcoming legacy systems and of new necessary complements) of a significant number of users. If it does not, then nothing will happen.

  If a forecast expects people to change their ways or their products, it must be able to show why a new solution offers a leap in utility for them. If it expects mass market adoption, it must show why the adoption benefits a mass of people. Any forecast that cannot show that a change or innovation will raise total utility for a significantly large or otherwise powerful set of stakeholders is a forecast doomed to fail.

- **Are there proposing or opposing stakeholders, particularly powerful individuals and powerful organizations?** Any change, whether it is a new product, new legislation, or new industry standard, or any other factor, will be good for some stakeholders and less good for others. People or groups who stand to lose will oppose the change, and often the future turns on how well or how long they can oppose forces for change. New technology, particularly, often threatens to change the balance of power in an industry or in society. A good forecast will contain some form of stakeholder analysis, at a minimum identifying key actors and their interests and expected actions in support or against the forecast outcomes. It will anticipate new stakeholders or interest groups that may arise to defend existing interests.

- **Does the forecast challenge social, cultural, or moral norms?** A change will be blocked if it goes against prevailing cultural norms and values. Most modern societies tolerate a wide diversity of opinion and are host to many cultures and traditions, so some latitude can be expected. However, there are also common minimum standards that shift very slowly, if at all. Medical and genetic innovations, for example, run directly into these blockers, and the future in this realm will be determined less by what technology can do than what morality can tolerate.

- **Whose side is the law on?** Interests of particular groups in society, and society as a whole, are protected by law. The law is almost always, by design, a drag on the future. Lawmakers and judges get to weigh consideration of different stakeholders and can be expected to act conservatively. Sometimes a law or a legal principle is a direct blocker of change, for example where an innovation is possible but may be blocked by patent protection or the fear of liability suits.

- **Is the forecaster in love with the technology?** Technology is being developed all the time. It very rarely gets to market, let alone broad adoption and commercial success. This tells us that technology's whiz-bang capability is only a tiny piece in the puzzle of how the future will play out. If the forecaster exhibits evidence of a love affair with a particular new technology, or new technology in general, the forecast should be taken with a pinch of salt. Technophiles have a history of seeing big change when none is likely and rapid change when slow is likely.

The forecast that goes beneath the trends, to deducing from them what forces are acting on the status quo, will be able to consider the strength and durability of forward drivers in the light of competing forces that may change, nullify, or reverse them, thus changing, nullifying, or reversing the trend. It will be ready for breaks and reversals in trends as underlying forces play out against each other. If arguing that a trend will continue at present trajectory, it will show why its underlying drivers will win through.

Does the forecast underestimate the time to product emergence? Does it overestimate the pace at which people's habits change?

Historically, it has taken on average twenty years for technologies to move from the lab to full commercial status, and there is no indication that this time is getting shorter. It could even get longer with ever-higher legislative and licensing requirements. A poor forecast will assume that significantly new technology or application will become available in months or years instead of decades. If there is a reason to think adoption and diffusion will take less time than average, the forecaster should bring evidence, and the forecast consumer should treat it with skepticism.

Part of the reason forecasts overestimate the emergence of change is because they overestimate peoples' propensity to change and their rate of change. If change requires users to do things differently, learn new skills, or make new purchases, then this change must be expected to take a long time. It is safe to assume that old ways will change reluctantly and that people would rather graft a new capability onto their old habits than adopt the new.

Does the forecaster assume change? Does the forecast underestimate the full hump change must overcome? Does the forecaster recognize what doesn't change?

If there are no convincing reasons for a development, the forecaster should assume the status quo continues. A future different from today implies that forces of change will have overcome blocking forces, and a good forecast will adequately explain how a shift in the balance of power between drivers and blockers supports the prediction.

Good forecasting is as much about seeing what *won't* change in the future. Even in fast-moving situations, not everything will change. In fact, many human and social needs and aspirations are timeless. From the Bible to Greek mythology to Chaucer to our era, much is similar in how humans see themselves and how they behave in families and institutions. Breathless shock-of-the-new forecasts are quick to assert that biotechnology or the Internet, or 9/11, or China's emergence, etc., "changes everything." This may sell magazines, but smart thinking says much in the human realm will stay the same.

Further Reading

The field of forecasting and future studies is vast. This partial list focuses just on key texts helpful in assessing forecasts and works specifically mentioned in the text.

Ascher, W., *Forecasting: An Appraisal for Policy Makers and Planners* (Baltimore: Johns Hopkins University Press, 1978).

Bell, W., *Foundations of Futures Studies* (Edison, NJ: Transaction Press, 1996).

Chan Kim, W., & Mauborgne, R., "Charting Your Company's Future." *Harvard Business Review* (May-June, 2002).

Clarke, I.F., *The Pattern of Expectation 1644-2001* (London: Jonathan Cape, 1979).

Courtney, H. et al., "Strategy Under Uncertainty," *Harvard Business Review* (November-December, 1997).

Courtney, H., *20/20 Foresight* (Boston: HBS Press, 2001).

Day, G., & Schoemaker, P., "Scanning the Periphery." *Harvard Business Review* (November-December, 2005).

De Geus, A., *The Living Company* (Boston: HBS Press, 1997).

Duncan, N., "Why Can't We Predict?" *New Scientist*, *136*(1841) (October, 1992).

Gibbons, P. L., "The Forecast Filter." *AMS Catalyst* (Spring, 2002).

Glenn, J., & Gordon, T. (Eds.), *Futures Research Methodology, v2.0* (CD-ROM) (New York: American Council for the United Nations University, Millennium Project, 2003).

Hamel, G., & Prahalad, C.K., *Competing for the Future* (Boston: HBS Press, 1994).

Hamel, G., & Prahalad, C.K., "Strategic Intent." *Harvard Business Review* (May-June, 1989).

Hines, A., "A Checklist for Evaluating Forecasts." *The Futurist* (November-December, 1995).

Hines, A., & Bishop, P., *Thinking about the Future, Guidelines for Strategic Foresight* (Washington, DC: Social Technologies, 2007).

James, J., *Thinking in the Future Tense* (New York: Simon & Schuster, 1996).

Jervis, R., *Systemic Effects* (Princeton, NJ: Princeton University Press, 1997).

Kleiner, A., "The Man Who Saw the Future." *Strategy+Business* (Spring, 2003).

Kleiner, A., "Consequential Heresies." *Global Business Network* (1989).

Kleiner, A., "The End of the Official Future." *Garbage Magazine* (March-April, 1992).

Liotta, P., & Somes, T., "The Art of Reperceiving." *Naval War College Review* (Autumn, 2003).

Mahaffie, J., "Why Forecasts Fail." *American Demographics* (March, 1995).

Paulos, J.A., *A Mathematician Reads the Newspaper* (New York: Basic Books, 1996).

Rittel, H., & Webber, M., "Dilemmas in a General Theory of Planning." *Policy Sciences, 4* (1973).

Rogers, E., *Diffusion of Innovations* (New York: Free Press, 1962).

Schnaars, S., *Megamistakes* (New York: Free Press, 1989).

Schwartz, P., *The Art of the Long View* (New York: Doubleday, 1991).

Schwartz, P., Leyden, P., & Hyatt, J., *The Long Boom: A Vision for the Coming Age of Prosperity* (New York: Perseus Publishing, 1999).

Sherden, W., *The Fortune Sellers* (New York: John Wiley & Sons, 1998).

Scott Armstrong, J., *Long-Range Forecasting*, 2nd ed. (New York: John Wiley & Sons, 1985).

Seidensticker, B., *Futurehype: The Myths of Technology Change* (San Francisco: BK Books, 2006).

Slaughter, R., *The Knowledge Base of Futures Studies* (Foresight International, 2005).

van der Heijden, K., *Scenarios: The Art of Strategic Conversation* (New York: John Wiley & Sons, 2005).

van der Heijden, K., Bradfield, R., Burt, G., Cairns, G., & Wright, G., *The Sixth Sense* (New York: John Wiley & Sons, 2002).

Wachs, M., "When Planners Lie with Numbers." *Journal of the American Planning Association, 55* (1989).

Wachs, M., "Forecasting vs Envisioning," *Journal of the American Planning Association, 67* (2001).

Wack, P., "Scenarios: Unchartered Waters Ahead." *Harvard Business Review* (September-October, 1985).

Wack, P., "Scenarios: Shooting the Rapids." *Harvard Business Review* (November-December, 1985).

Walt, S., "The Hidden Nature of Systems." *The Atlantic Monthly* (September, 1998).

Weiner, E., & Brown A., *An Insider's Guide to the Future* (New York: WEB, 1997).

Weiner, E., & Brown, A., *Future Think* (Upper Saddle River, NJ: Prentice Hall, 2005).

Index

A
Accelerations, anticipating, 190–91
Airline travel industry, 113, 114–15
Alternative futures, point forecasts *versus*, 23–24
Amazon, 12
Assumptions
  errors, 58
  forecast filtering and, 276–77
  forecasting and, 203–5
  identifying and testing, 102–3
  questioning, 99–101
AT&T, 13
Authors, reputation of, 79–80

B
Balancing loops, 180–81
Barnum effect, 92
Best, Joel, 43, 56
Bias
  confirmation, 91
  conscious, 68
  forecast, probing for, 77–78
  forecast filtering and, 270–72
  futurist's, 76–77
  herd, 92
  human, 91–92
  judgmental heuristics, 91–93
  media situation, 74–75
  natural *versus* intentional, 64–66
  reputation of author and organization, 79–80
  situational, 92
  social, 91–92
  technophile, 77
  traps, 66–77
  zeitgeist, 93–97
Bias-prone contexts, 66–77, 271–72
  election and government forecasts, 71
  funding, foresight and, 69–70
  insider forecasts, 72–74
  internal, motivational forecasts, 68–69
  publicity and, 71–72
  self-asserted forecasts, 67–68
  sponsored forecasts, 70–71
Blockers, 142, 147
  forecast filtering and, 278–83
Brain, information filtering and, 88–90
Brave New World (Huxley), 35

C
Capital One, 12
Capital turns, 43
Carson, Rachel, 34
Causal loop diagrams, 183–84

Causation, correlation *versus*, 57–58
Change
    drivers, 141
    forecasting and, 5–7
    limits of, 188–90
    organizations and, 144
    pace of, 147–48
    status quo and, 148–49
    technology and, 143–44
    values and, 145
Chaos theory, 160
CIA, forecasting by, 8
Cisco, 165
Complexity, forecast filtering and, 274–76
Confirmation bias, 92
Conscious bias, 68
Consumer
    change and, 128–31
    power, role of, 109–11
    utility, role of, 114–15
Context, detachment of, 46
Cornucopians, 32
Corporate genetics, 73
Correlation, causation *versus*, 57–58
Crises, avoiding, 12–13
Critical mass, 186–87
Critique of Pure Reason (Kant), 86

D

Damned Lies and Statistics (Best), 43
Data
    assumption errors, 58
    correlation *versus* causation, 57–58
    definition validity, 50–54
    Delphi studies, 54–55
    demographic, 48
    extrapolation, 30
    improper use of, 57–58
    inference and, 57
    innumeracy, 56–57
    measurement of, 42–43
    number skepticism, practicing, 58–60
    omission of, 65
    outdated, 48
    projected, 49
    quality of, 41, 44–60
    reliability issues, 44–60
    sample validity, 49–50
    scenarios and, 207–8
    secondary, 44–48
    selective choice of, 65
    survey, 54–55
    triangulation of, 59
    unreported, 55–56
Decision heuristics, 91
Definition validity, 50–54
    definitions across places and situations, 53–54
    definitions across time, 51–53
    loose definitions, 50–51
    standardization, lack of, 53
de Geus, Arie, 204
Delays, anticipating, 190–91
Delphi studies, 30, 54–55, 97
Dementia forecast, 235–41
Demographic data, outdated, 48
Department of Defense, 80
Determinism, limits of, 159–65
Diffusion of Innovations (Rogers), 129
Diminishing marginal returns, 111–14
Driver-level analysis, 145–50
Drivers, forecast filtering and, 278–83
Dystopias, 30, 35–36

E

Economies of scale, 122
Election forecasts, 71
Emotional words, bias and, 65–66
Enabler, 141
Enron, 52
Erlich, Paul, 33, 34
Errors
    assumption, 58
    forecasting, 13
    hypothesis, 51
    type I, 51
    type II, 51
Evaluation, model for, 19
Expectations, forecast, 200–201
Expert forecasts, 97–99
Exponential change view, 192–94

F

False positives, 51
Feedback loops, 182
Filtering, of forecasts, 13–15

INDEX ◊ 291

Ford, Henry, 12
Forecast filtering
    applying, 217–62
    assumptions and paradigm paralysis, 276–77
    complexity, managing, 274–76
    drivers and blockers, 278–83
    information quality, 269–70
    interpretation and bias, 270–72
    methods and models, 272–73
    quantitative limits, 273–74
    specificity in, 267–69
    summary of steps, 265–83
    zeitgeist and Groupthink, 277–78
Forecasts
    anticipating for virtuous cycles, 187–88
    benefits of, 25
    bias, probing for, 77–78
    editorial oversight, lack of, 75–76
    election and government, 71
    errors in, 13
    evaluating, 9
    expectations, 200–201
    expert, 97–99
    filtering, 13–15
    future-aligning, 24–19, 266–67
    future and, 5–7
    future-influencing, 24–29, 266–67
    insider, 72–74
    internal, motivational, 68–69
    learning from, 11–13
    long-medium, 20, 22
    long-term, 20–21, 22
    optimistic *versus* pessimistic, 32–34
    origins of, 7–9
    period, 19, 20–23
    point, 23–24
    political aspects of, 63–81
    poor, 9–11
    primary data and, 44
    publicity and, 71–72
    purpose of, 266
    qualitative, 168
    scenario planning, 201–3
    self-asserted, 67–68
    short-medium, 20, 22
    short-term, 20, 22
    skepticism, 11
    sponsored, 70–71
    standardization, lack of, 4–5
    technology-push, 116–21
    ultra-long term, 21
    validity of, 4–5
    zeitgeist bias in, 93–97
Foresight, determining approach, 168–71
Forrester Research, 8, 80
Foucault, Michel, 86
Fraud, 52
Friction, 141, 147
Funding, foresight and, 69–70
Future-aligning forecasts, 41, 266–67
    future-influencing *versus*, 24–29
    identifying, 30–31
Future-influencing forecasts, 41, 266–67
    extremes of, 35–36
    future-aligning *versus*, 24–29
    goals, 28–29
    identifying, 30–31
    intentional bias and, 66
    power and politics and, 36

G

Gartner Inc., 8, 80
Gates, Bill, 12
General Motors, 73
Google, 73
Government forecasts, 71
Groupthink, 277–78

H

Hamel, Gary, 73
Herd bias, 92
Hitler, Adolf, 36
Housing and mortgage finance forecast, 219–25
Human bias, 91–92
Hypothesis
    errors, 51
    testing, 51

I

IBM, 12
IMF, 8
Inference, data and, 57
Inflection points, 145–47

Information, filtering, 88–90
Innumeracy, 56–57
Insider forecasts, 72–74
Intentional bias
  data, omission of, 65
  emotional words, 65–66
  natural *versus,* 64–66
  prejudicial definition of key terms, 66
  prejudicial organization and emphasis, 65
  worse case examples and, 66
Interactions, 163
Internal forecasts, 68–69

K
Kahn, Herman, 201
Kant, Immanuel, 86
Kelleher, Herb, 12, 115
Kuhn, Thomas, 87

L
Lag, 163
Law of diminishing returns, 111, 112
Legal profession forecast, 243–47
The Living Company (de Geus), 204
Lobbying, 25
The Long Boom (Schwartz), 96
Long-medium forecasts, 20, 22
Long-term forecasts, 20–21, 22
Loops
  balancing, 180–81
  feedback, 182
  reinforcing, 179–80

M
Malthus, Thomas, 33
Malthusianism, 33
Managerial frames, 73
Marginal utility, 111–14
Market utility analysis, 119
Mattel, 73
Measurement, of data, 42–43
Media
  editorial oversight, lack of, 75–76
  forecasting and, 7
  quality, 74
  secondary data and, 47–48
  situation biases, 74–75

Mein Kampf (Hitler), 36
Microsoft, 12
Model for evaluation, building, 19
Multiple futures approach, 23–24

N
Narrative, scenarios and, 207–8
National Bureau of Economic Research, 8
Natural bias, intentional *versus,* 64–66
Nike, 12
1984 (Orwell), 35
Nokia, 12
Number laundering, 46–47
Number skepticism, practicing, 58–60

O
Obesity forecast, 241–43
Optimistic forecasts, 32–34
  data and, 41
Optimistic stretch forecast policy, 69
The Order of Things (Foucault), 86
Organizations
  change and, 144
  nonprofit, 69
  reputation of, 79–80
Oscillations, anticipating, 191–92
Outdated data, 48

P
Pan Am, 12
Paradigm shifts, 90
Parker Bros, 73
Paulos, John Allen, 56
Pendulum swings, anticipating, 191–92
Period, of forecasts, 19, 20–23
Pessimistic forecasts, 32–34
  data and, 41
Point forecasts, 23–24
  alternative futures *versus,* 23–24
Political aspects, of forecasting, 63–81
  author and organization, reputation of, 79–80
  bias-prone context and bias traps, 66–77
  natural *versus* intentional bias, 64–66
  political questions, posing, 77–78
Politics, forecasting and, 36
The Population Bomb (Erlich), 33

Power, forecasting and, 36
Prahalad, C.K., 73
Prediction markets forecasting technique, 67, 81
Predictive statements, 3
Prejudicial definitions, of key terms, 66
Prejudicial organizations, 65
Price elasticity, 124
Primary data, 44
Probability, misunderstanding, 56
Projected data, 49
Publicity, bias and, 71–72

Q

Qualitative forecasts, 168
Quality
 of data, 44–60
 information, 269–70
 utility principle and, 123
Quantitative modeling, 156–58
Quantitative studies, 58–59

R

Rand Corporation, 201
Reliability, of data, 44–60
Resistance, change *versus,* 148
Return on investment, 25
Rogers, Everett, 129
Royal Dutch Shell, 8, 201

S

Sample validity, 49–50
Scenario planning, 201–3
 assumptions and, 203–5
 data and narrative, 207–8
 limits of, 211–12
 scenarios, creating, 205–7
 testbeds in, 208–9
 visionary scenarios, 210–11
Schwartz, Peter, 96
S-curves, 188–90
Secondary data, 44–48
 detachment of context, 46
 detachment of statistical caveats, 45–46
 media and, 47–48

 number laundering, 46–47
 repetition and, 47
Self-asserted forecasts, 67–68
Shape, 163
Short-medium forecasts, 20, 22
Short-term forecasts, 20, 22
Siemens, 8
The Silent Spring (Carson), 34
Simon, Julian, 34
Situational bias, 92
Skepticism
 forecast, 11
 number, 58–60
Social bias, 91–92
Southwest Airlines, 12, 115
Space travel, 121–22
Specificity, in forecast filtering, 267–69
Sponsored forecasts, 70–71
Stagflation, 121
Standardization, lack of in definitions, 53
Statistical analysis, quantitative modeling and, 156–58
Statistical caveats, detachment of, 45–46
Statistics, sampling in, 49–50
The Structure of Scientific Revolutions (Kuhn), 87
Success, in forecasting, 11–13
Survey data, 54–55
 design methods, 54–55
Systems, 176–94
 accelerations and delays, anticipating, 190–91
 balancing loops, 180–81
 causal loop diagrams, 183–84
 causes and effects, charting, 181–83
 critical mass and tipping points, 186–87
 exponential change view, 192–94
 modeling, 178–79
 oscillations and pendulum swings, anticipating, 191–92
 personal behavior and, 184–85
 reinforcing loops, 179–80
 S-curves and limits of change, 188–90

T

Technology, 6
 change and, 143–44
Technology-push forecasting, 116–21

Techno-optimists, 32
Technophile bias, 77
Thresholds, 163
Time-series analysis, 157
Tipping points, 186–87
Totalitarianism, 35
Trends
    breaks, 146–47
    defined, 136–37
    driver-level analysis and, 145–50
    extrapolation of, 141–45
    projecting, 139–41
    recognition problems, 138–39
    systematic interactions and, 149–50
    tracking, 137–38
Triangulation, of data, 59
Truth, subjectivity of, 86–88
Type I errors, 51
Type II errors, 51

U

Ultra-long term forecasts, 21
Uncertainty, distinguishing levels of, 165–67
Unreported data, 55–56
U.S. Congressional Budget Office, 8
USDA agricultural forecast, 248–62
US News and World Report, 46
Utility analysis, 110
Utility principle, 122–28
    consumer preferences and, 123
    economies of scale, 122
    groups in, 124
    innovation and, 126
    old products in, 127–28
    price elasticity, 124–25
    prices and, 125–26
    quality and, 123
    social values, 125
Utopias, 30, 35–36

V

Validity
    definition, 50–54
    sample, 49–50
Vicious cycles, 179–80
Virtual technology, 28
Virtuous cycles, 179–80
    stimulating, 187–88
Visionary scenarios, 210–11

W

Wal-Mart, 12
The Washington Post, 73
West Virginia correctional population forecast, 226–35
World Bank, 8, 28
Worst case examples, bias and, 66

X

Xerox, 129

Y

Yellow Pages, 73
Y2K disaster, 9–10, 27

Z

Zeitgeist bias, 93–97, 277–78

Printed in the USA
CPSIA information can be obtained
at www.ICGtesting.com
JSHW030726220324
59652JS00010B/250